MEL BAY'S COMPLETE BOOK OF EXERCISES FOR THE PIANIST

BY GAIL SMITH

FOREWORD

When Sir Isaac Newton was asked how he discovered the Law of Gravitation, he replied, "By always thinking about it." If your goal is to become a great pianist, you must put action behind the thought and exercise your fingers.

Each exercise in this book is important for your fingers and hands. These exercises will provide an essential finger workout program for every pianist.

First practice every exercise slowly. Then increase the speed.

If you know a thing, it's simple; if it's not simple, you don't know it.

Because eyes as well as hands play the piano, the first exercise is a Palindrome I composed for this exercise book. There are 120 measures that are to be played backwards as well as forwards. The eyes are exercised when you read backwards in this way, which helps in developing your sight-reading. There IS more to this Palindrome exercise than meets the eye. It is the ultimate exercise since it offers the only 120 combinations known for playing five notes. Yes, using the factorial table of notes, here are the possibilities going from two tones to twelve semi-tones:

    2 tones = 2
    3 tones = 6
    4 tones = 24
    5 tones = 120
    6 tones = 720
    7 tones = 5,040
    8 tones = 40,320
    9 tones = 362,880
    10 tones = 3,628,800
    11 tones = 39,916,800
    12 tones = 479,001,600

First, I found all the 120 ways you can play the five tones, and since we have five fingers, by playing this exercise you will be playing the only possible combinations known to man. I arranged the patterns into a Palindrome so that you will benefit your eyes as well as your fingers.

This is a new benchmark for exercise books. The most useful exercises of Hanon, Czerny, Chopin, Schmitt, Brahms, Philipp, Pischna, Clementi, William Mason, Frederic Wieck (the father of Clara Schumann), and others are combined for the first time creating *The Complete Book of Exercises for Pianists*.

Remember, only those who have the patience to do the simple things perfectly ever acquire the skill to do the difficult things easily.

Gail Smith

TABLE OF CONTENTS

FINGER WARM-UPS
by Gail Smith

Open and shut your hand twenty times, then stretch your hand open as wide as you can.

Stretch in between each of the fingers and gently pull them apart as far as they will go.

Massage the back of each hand.

Massage in between the ligaments of the fingers.

Pull the fingers gently backwards.

Wrap "Silly Putty" around two fingers at a time, then pull the fingers apart as the "Silly Putty" stretches like a rubber band. Your fingers will form the letter V.

Let the tips of your fingers press into a ball of "Silly Putty" as you keep your finger knuckles curved.

Form circles with your fingers as you press the thumb to the second finger five times (making circles), then the thumb to the third, the thumb to the fourth, and finally the thumb to the fifth finger (keeping the fingers rounded forming circles as you repeat with both hands).

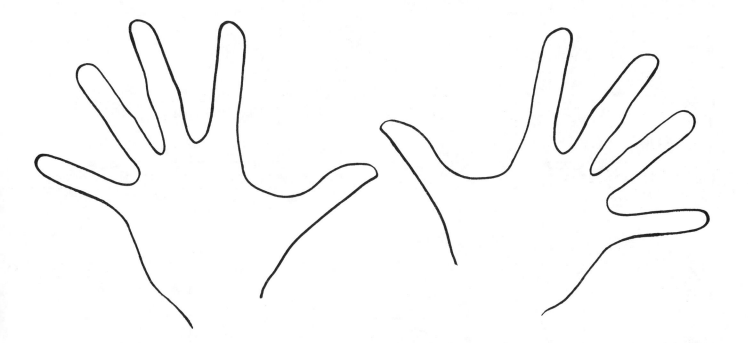

GAIL SMITH'S PALINDROME EXERCISE
5 FINGER PALINDROME 120

TWO FINGER EXERCISES - DIATONIC SCALE

William Mason

Exercise No. 1 First slow form. *The clinging legato touch.*

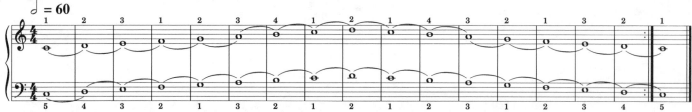

For the sake of abbreviation the exercises which follow are written out on the right hand part of the staff. The left hand plays uniformly one octave below the right, beginning on c of the small octave. Fingering above the notes for the right hand and below for the left.

No. 2 Second slow form *Clinging legato touch and Elastic touch in alternation.*

No. 3 Second slow form

To avoid crowding the plates the application of the other three pairs of fingers is here omitted, but on no account must they be neglected in practice.

No. 4 First moderato form

No. 5 First moderato form

No. 6 Second moderato form

No. 7 Second moderato form

EXERCISE - KEY OF C

Isidor Philipp

Exercise - Key of G

Isidor Philipp

ONE OCTAVE SCALE EXERCISE

Louis Köhler

Allegro

15

HANON'S TWENTY EXERCISES

No. 1

Stretch between the fifth and fourth fingers of the left hand in ascending and the fifth and fourth fingers of the right hand in descending.

For studying the 20 exercises in this First Part, begin with the metronome set at 60, gradually increasing the speed up to 108; this is the meaning of the double metronome-mark at the head of each exercise.

Lift the fingers high and with precision, playing each note very distinctly.

Charles Lewis Hanon

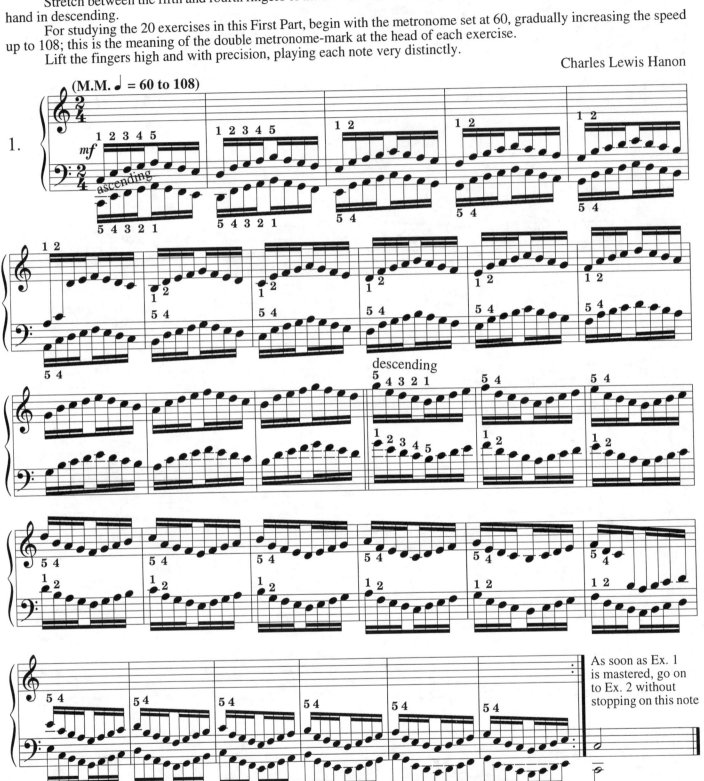

As soon as Ex. 1 is mastered, go on to Ex. 2 without stopping on this note

No. 2

(3-4) When this exercise is mastered, recommence the preceding one, and play both together four times without interruption; the fingers will gain considerably by practising these exercises, and those following, in this way.

(1) The fourth and fifth fingers being naturally weak, it should be observed that this exercise, and those following it are intended to render them as strong and agile as the second and third.

No. 3

(2-3-4) Before beginning to practise No. 3, play through the preceding exercises once or twice without stopping. When No. 3 is mastered, practise No. 4, and then No. 5, and as soon as they are thoroughly learned play through all three at least four times without interruption, not stopping until the last note. The entire work should be practised in this manner.

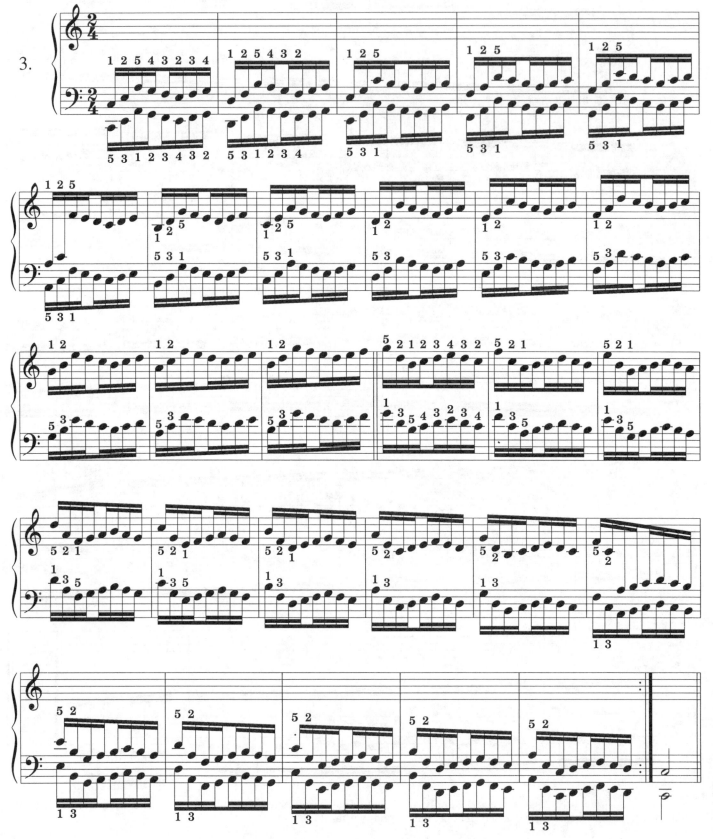

No. 4

(3-4-5) (1) Special exercise for the 3rd, 4th and 5th fingers of the hand.

No. 5

(1-2-3-4-5) We repeat, that the fingers should be lifted high, and with precision, until this entire volume is mastered.

(1) Preparation for the trill with the 4th and 5th fingers of the right hand.

No. 6

(5) To obtain the good results which we promise those who study this work, it is indispensable to play daily, at least once, the exercises already learned.

21

No. 7

(3-4-5) Exercise of the greatest importance for the 3rd, 4th and 5th fingers.

No. 8

(1-2-3-4-5) Very important exercise for all five fingers.

No. 9

Extension of the 4th and 5th, and general finger-exercise.

No. 10

(3-4) Preparation for the trill, for the 3rd and 4th fingers of the left hand in ascending (1); and for the 3rd and 4th of the right, descending (2).

No. 11

(3-4-5) Another preparation for the trill, for the 4th and 5th fingers.

No. 12

Extension of 1-5, and exercise for 3-4-5.

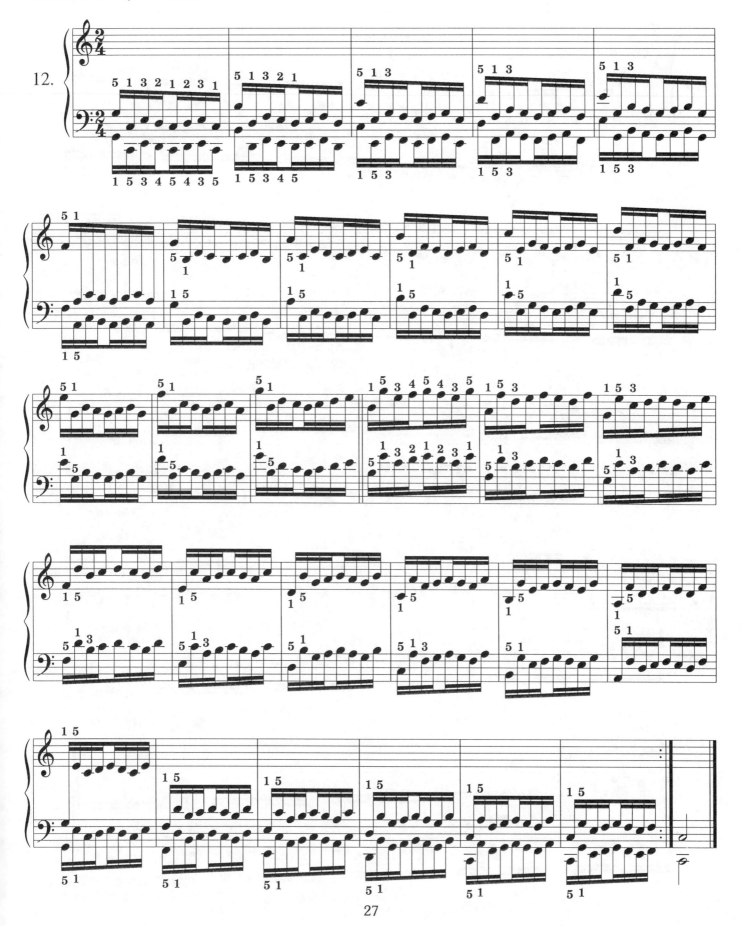

No. 13

No. 14

(3-4) Another preparation for the trill, for the 3rd and 4th fingers.

No. 15

Extension of 1-2, and exercise for all 5 fingers.

No. 16

Extension of 3-5, and exercise for 3-4-5.

No. 17

Extension of 1-2, 2-4, 4-5, and exercise for 3-4-5.

17.

No. 18

No. 19

No. 20

Extension of 2-4, 4-5, and exercise for 2-3-4.

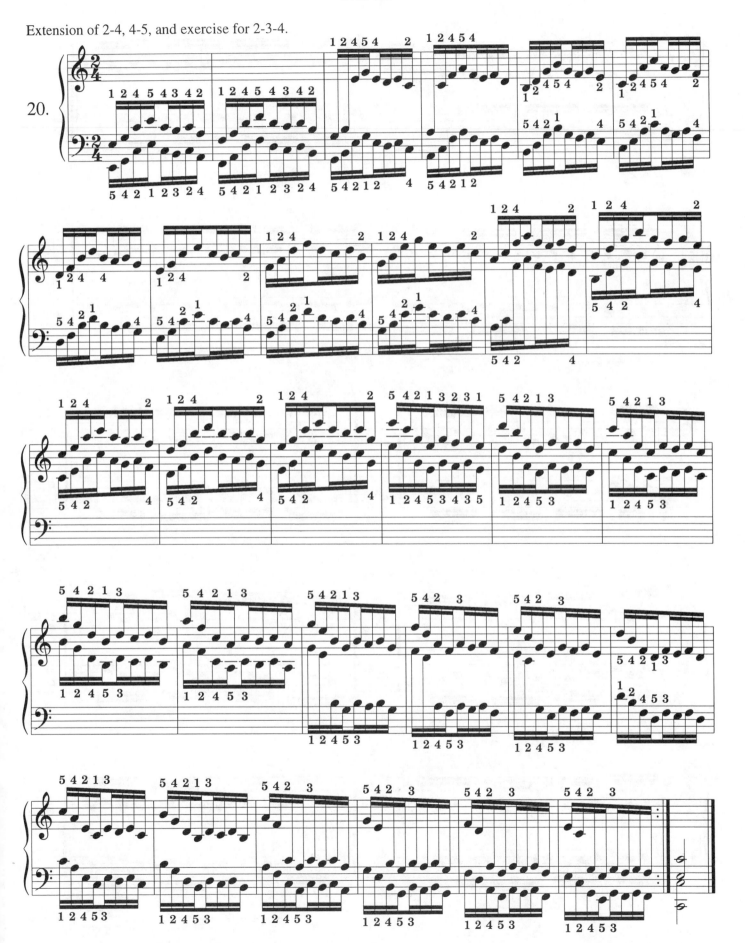

Schmitt's Exercises from Opus 16

A. Schmitt

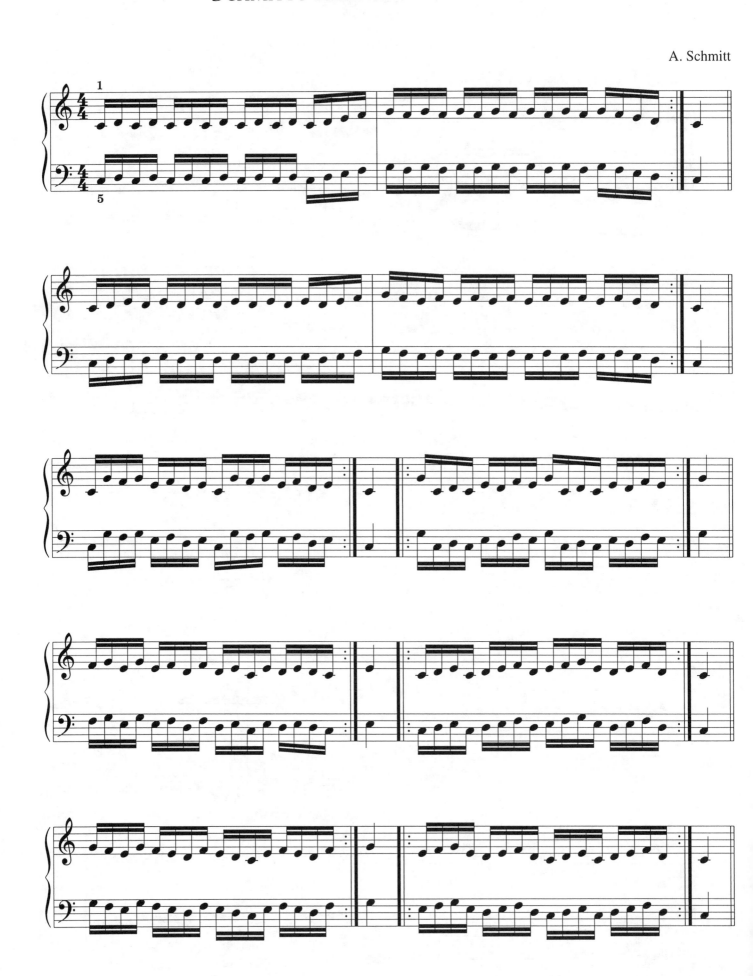

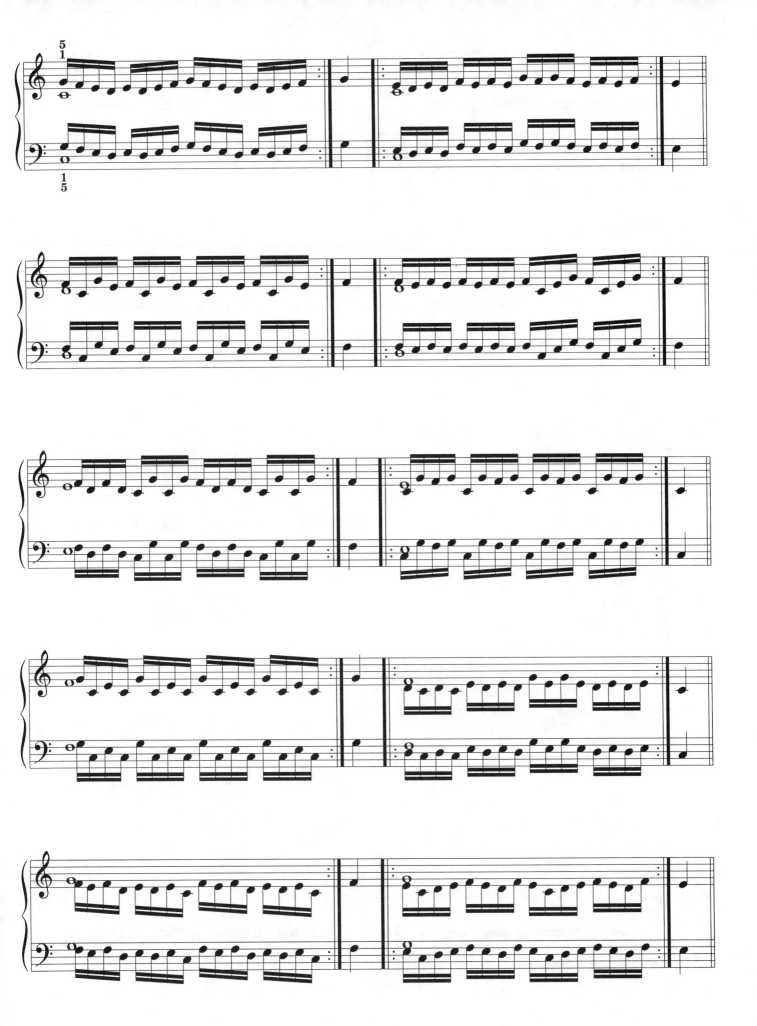

37

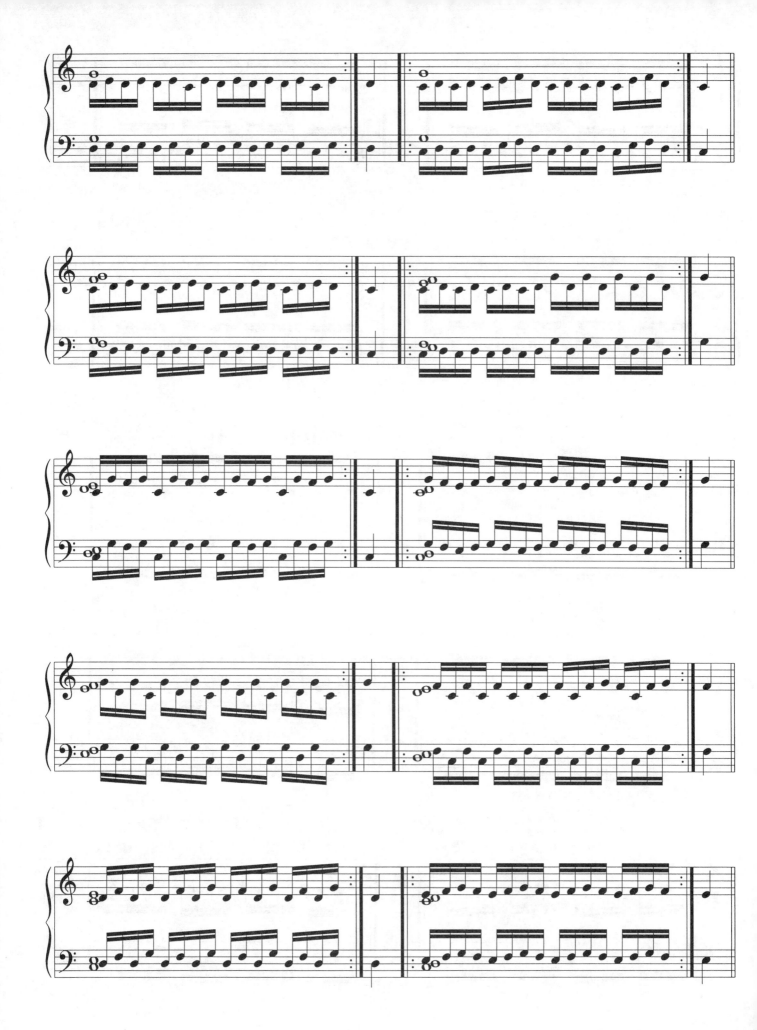

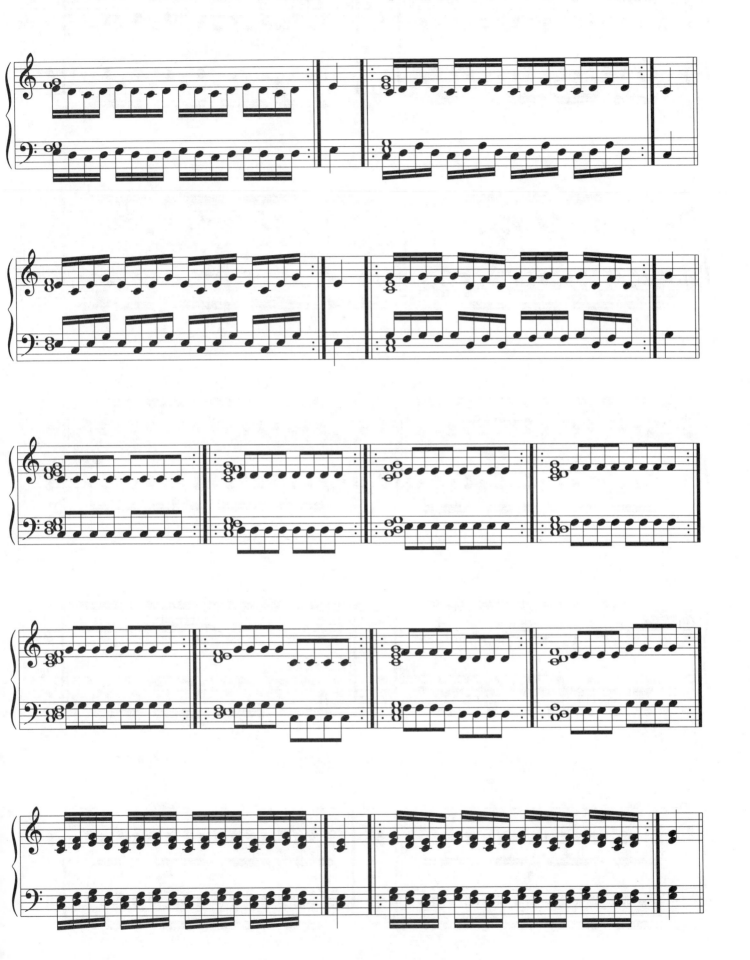

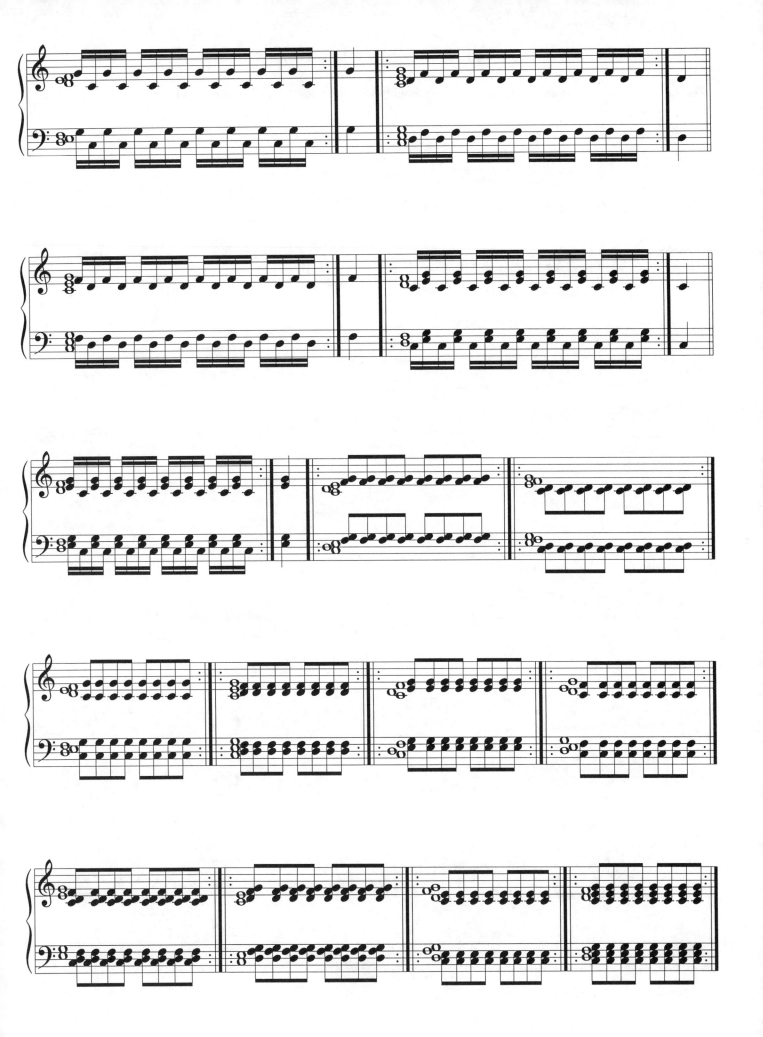

WEICK'S PIANO EXERCISES

These exercises were composed by Frederic Wieck who was Clara Schumann's father and her piano teacher.

Frederic Wieck

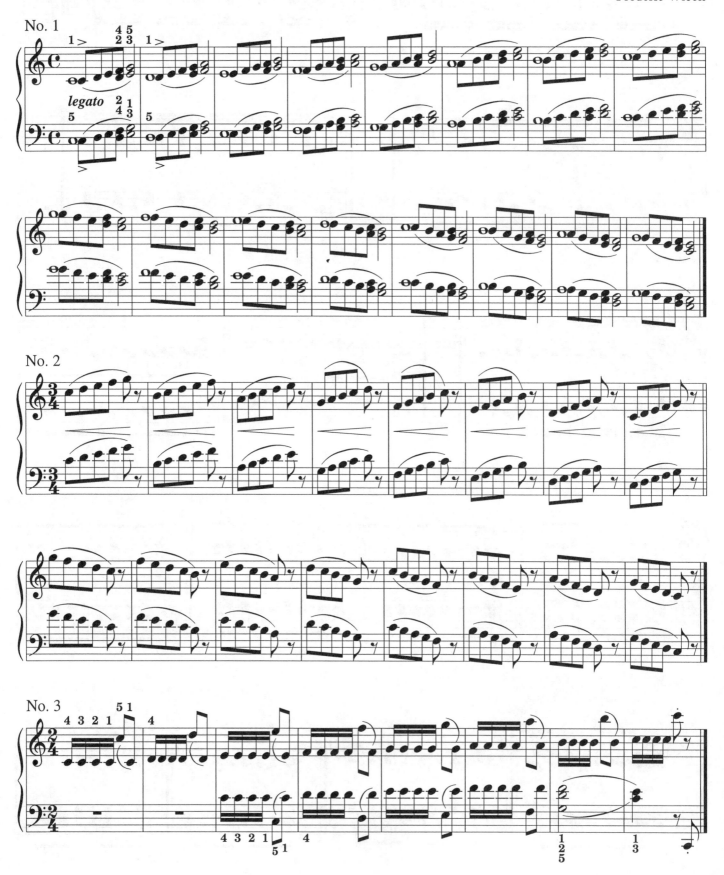

No. 4

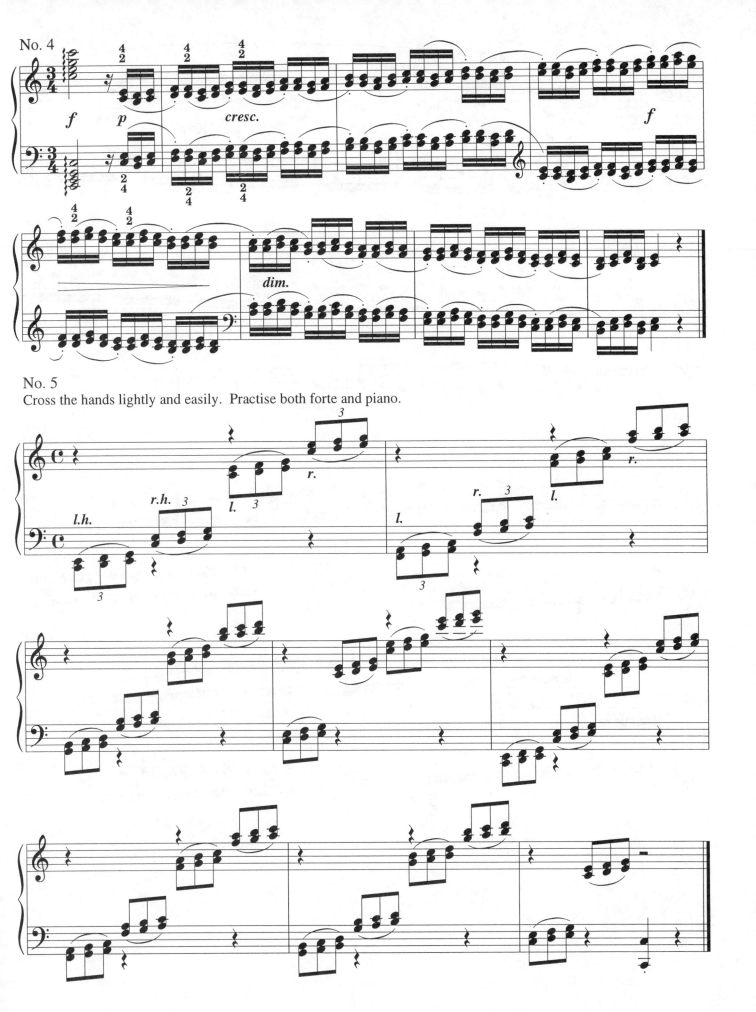

No. 5

Cross the hands lightly and easily. Practise both forte and piano.

No. 6

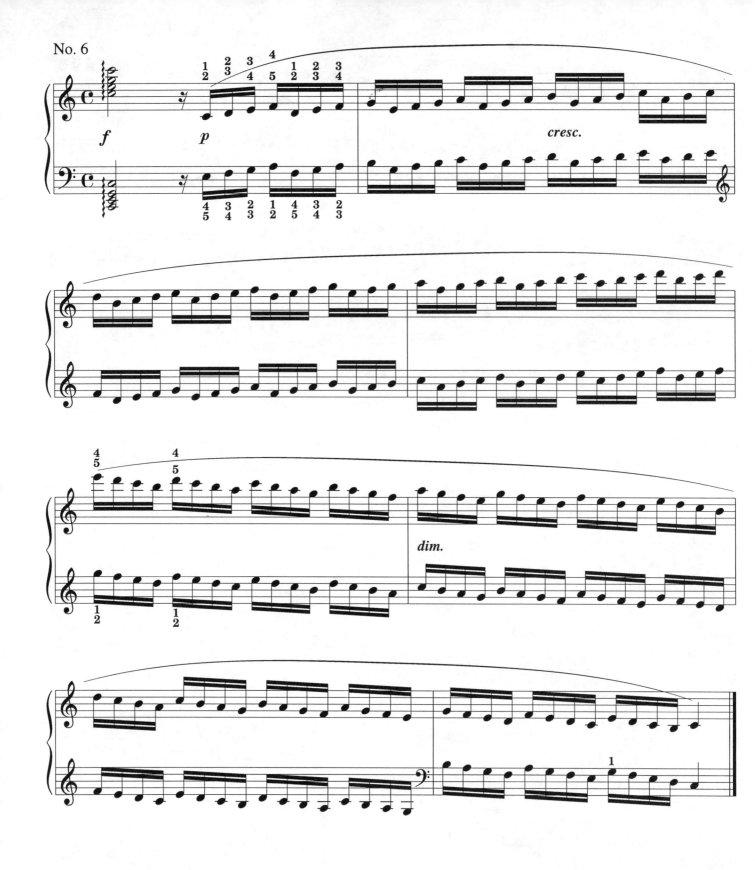

No. 7
The Triads, and Chords of the Seventh, of all major keys as a Study of the Arpeggio. Play evenly and with steady hand.

Frederic Wieck

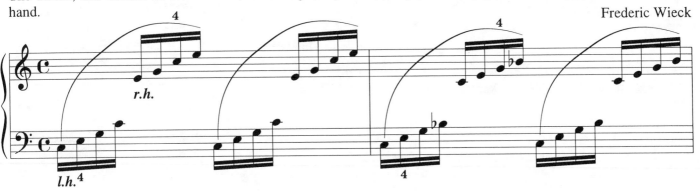

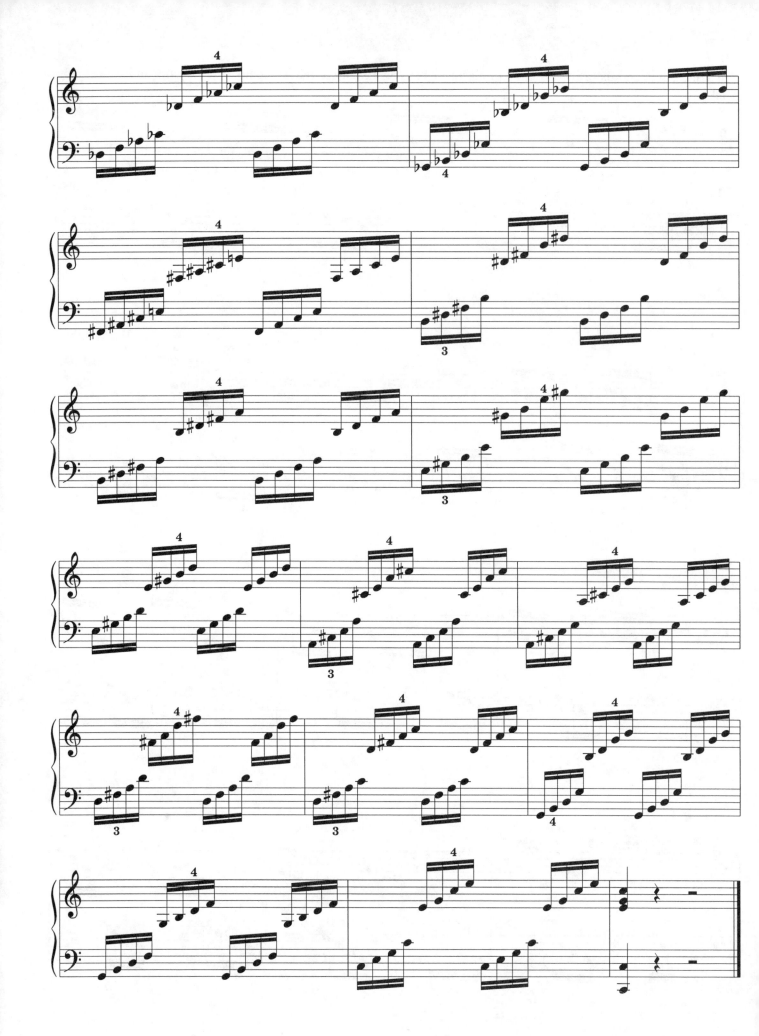

Frederic Wieck

TRILL EXERCISE

No. 9

Frederic Wieck

Study of the Trill with sustained notes.

Frederic Wieck

BRAHMS TRILL EXERCISE

Johannes Brahms

Repeating Note Rhythm Exercise Op. 4, No. 12

The following most valuable exercise in time must be practiced until it can be played through repeatedly without breaking the movement or varying the rate. Whatever dullness of rhythmic perception the pupil may manifest, the teacher must contrive to counteract by means of suitable planned exercises in rhythm. Those who have made practical acquaintance with Mason's tables of graded rhythms will have no difficulty here.

Krause

REPEATED SIXTEENTH NOTE EXERCISE

Carl Czerny

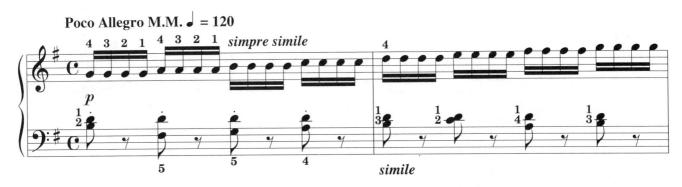

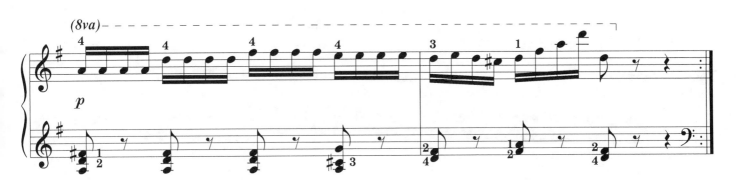

Exercises in Sixths

from Touch and Technic

by William Mason

Rotary Exercise in Sixths, for small hands.
For each hand alternately.

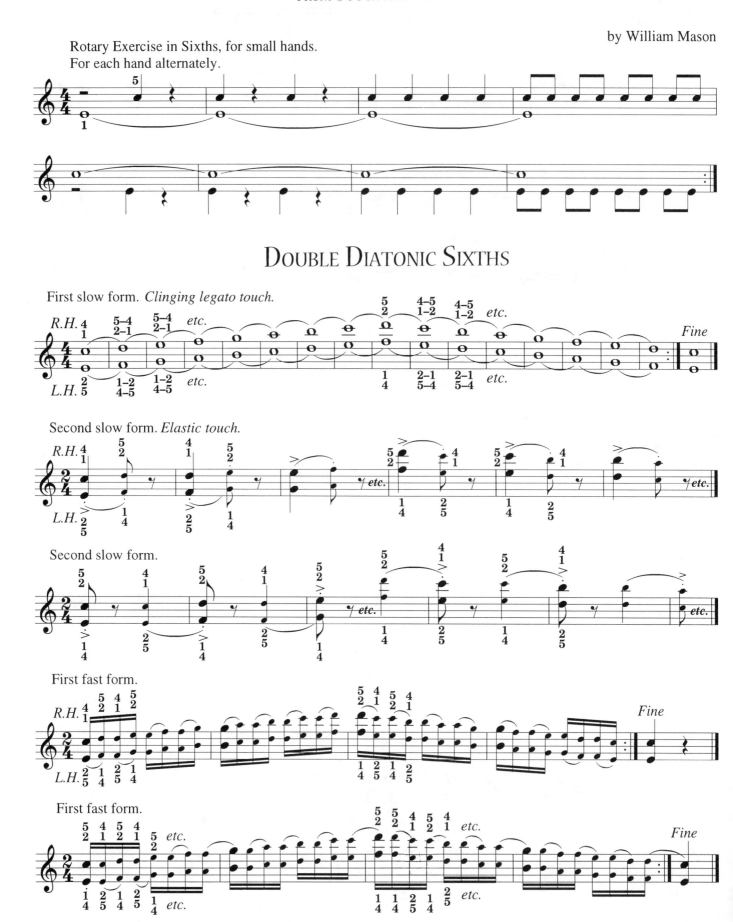

Double Diatonic Sixths

First slow form. *Clinging legato touch.*

Second slow form. *Elastic touch.*

Second slow form.

First fast form.

First fast form.

OCTAVE PRINCIPLES IN SIXTHS

(FOR SMALL HANDS ONLY)

William Mason

No. 1
Exercise for loosening wrist. First way.
The wrist sinking at the count "two."

No. 2
Exercise for loosening wrist. Second way.
The wrist sinking instantly that the touch is made.

Numbers 3 to 8 are varieties of light touch, each measure being played in the manner described
in Sec. 2, No. 3. Be sure that the manner therein described is observed and that while in the slower
forms the first tone may be somewhat accented, the later ones in the measure are all light and have
the character of echoes or reboundings of the first.

No. 3
Exercise for light touch, three tones to each impulse.

No. 4
Exercise for light touch, four tones to each impulse.

No. 5
The same touch, the hand moving with the bounding touches.
Observe the long intervals of repose, indicated by the rests.

No. 6
The same with shorter intervals of repose.

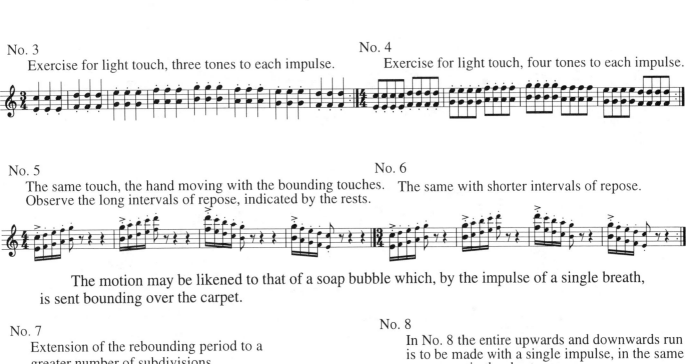

The motion may be likened to that of a soap bubble which, by the impulse of a single breath,
is sent bounding over the carpet.

No. 7
Extension of the rebounding period to a
greater number of subdivisions.

No. 8
In No. 8 the entire upwards and downwards run
is to be made with a single impulse, in the same
manner as in the shorter ones.

No. 9
A similar form involving thirds in ascending and
sixths in descending.

No. 10
The same applied to the left hand.
Be careful that the left wrist is kept in the same
condition as the right in the preceding exercise.

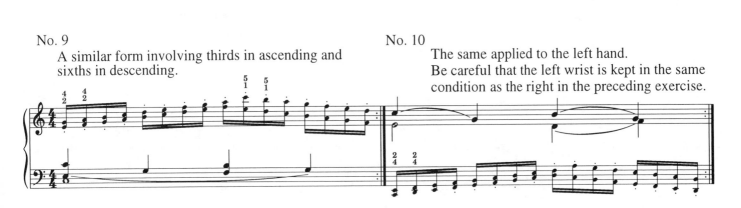

DAILY EXERCISE WITH WIDE STRETCHES

Hans Barth

L.H. one octave lower

FINGER WARM-UP

Johann Baptist Cramer

THE TWELVE MAJOR AND MINOR SCALES
(HARMONIC AND MELODIC)

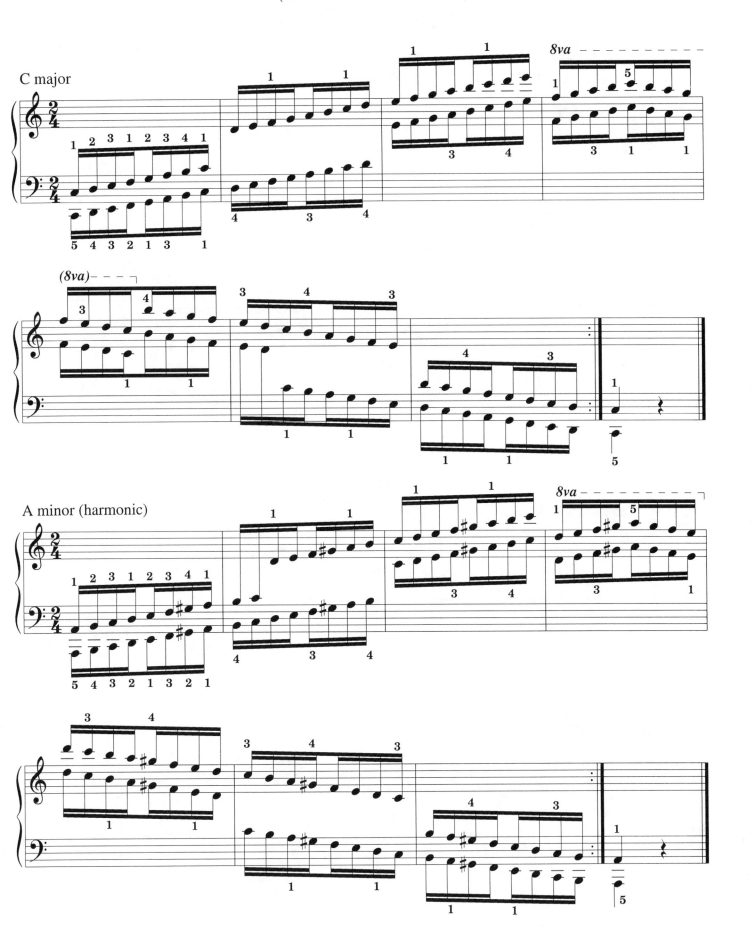

C major

A minor (harmonic)

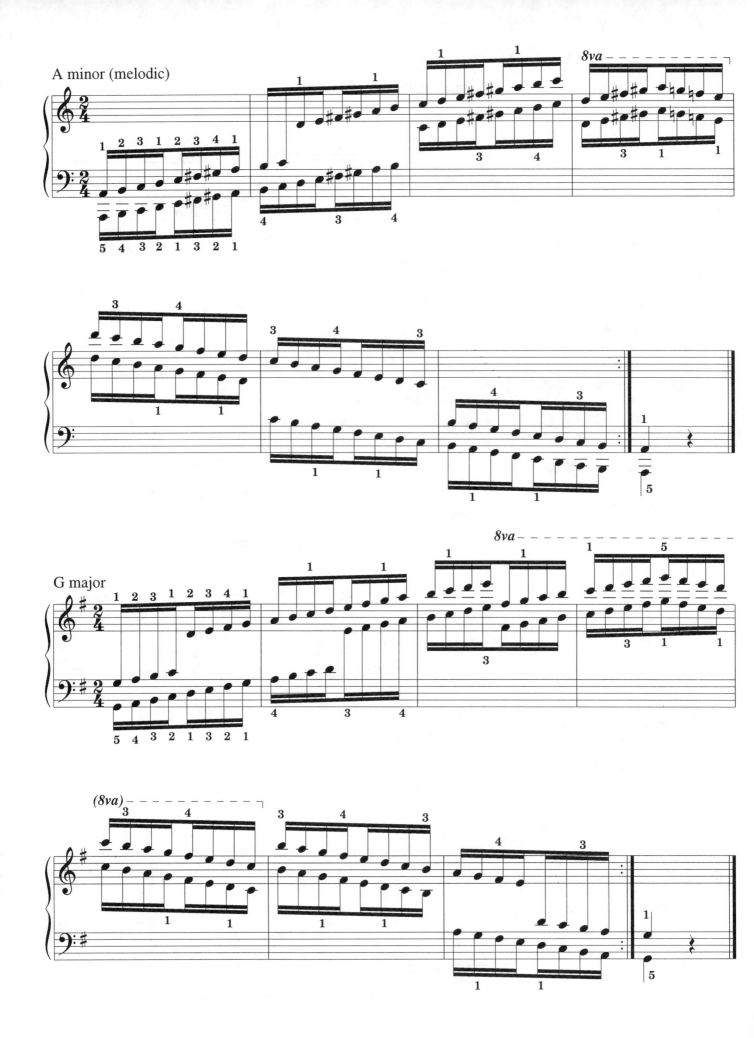

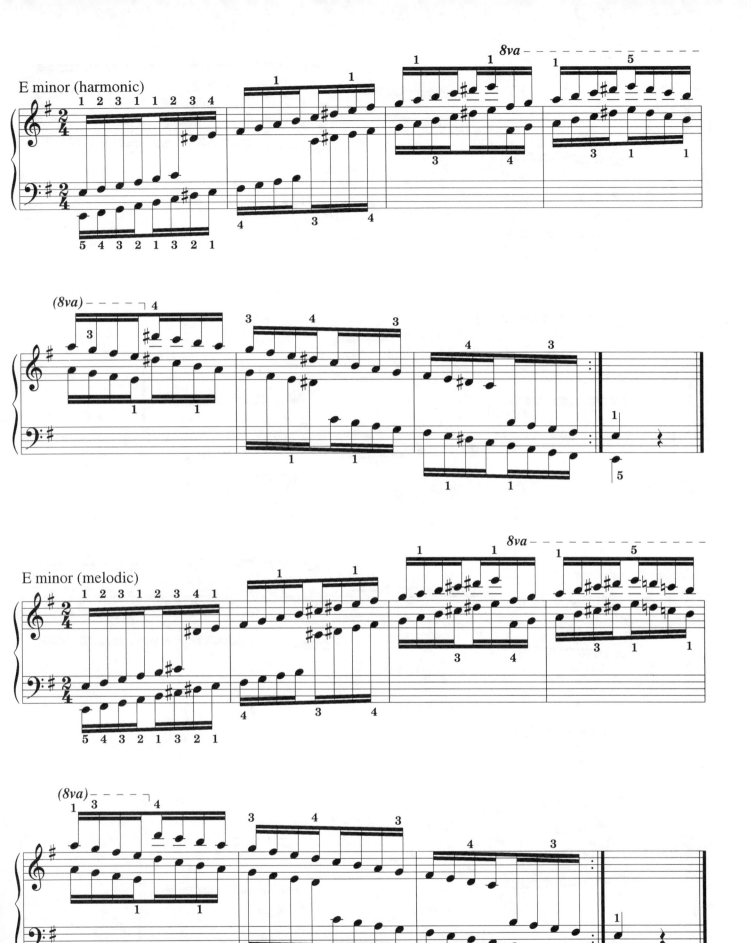

E minor (harmonic)

E minor (melodic)

D major

B minor (harmonic)

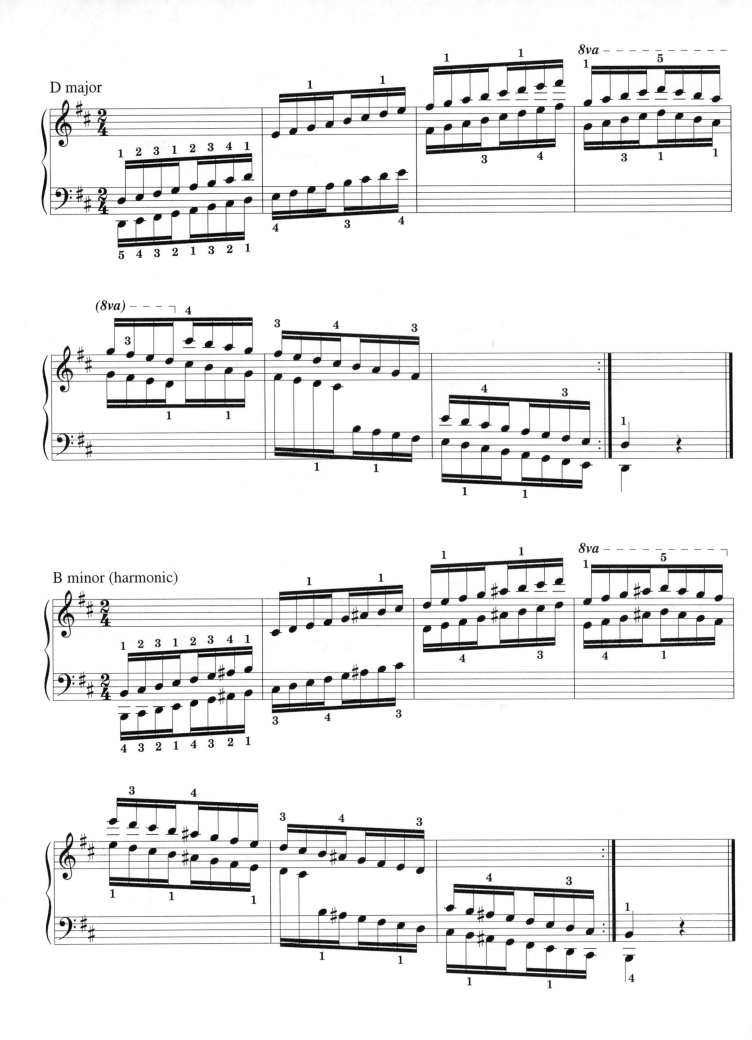

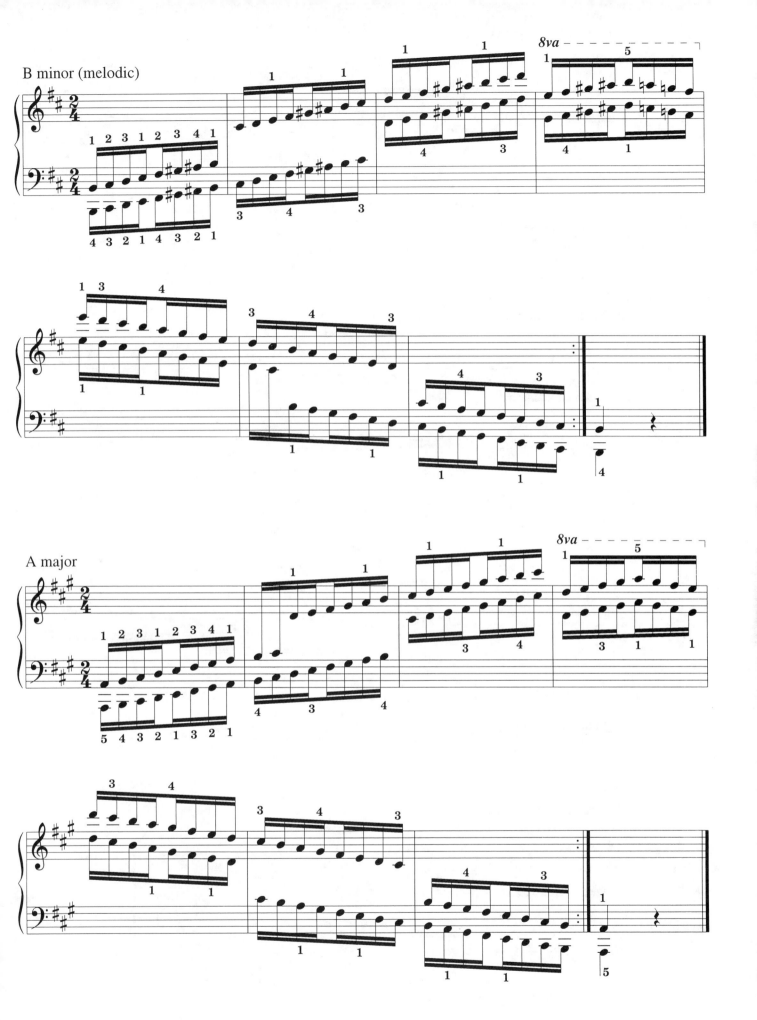

B minor (melodic)

A major

F# minor (harmonic)

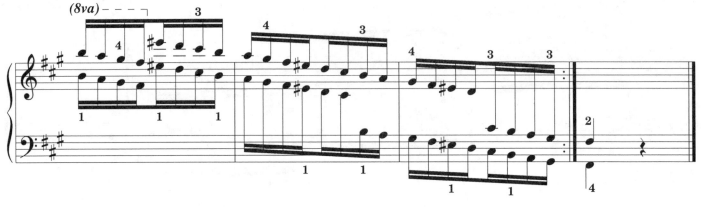

F# minor (melodic)

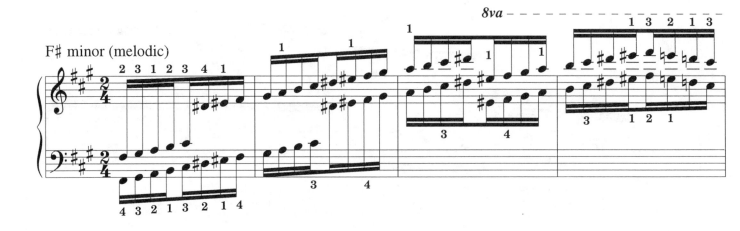

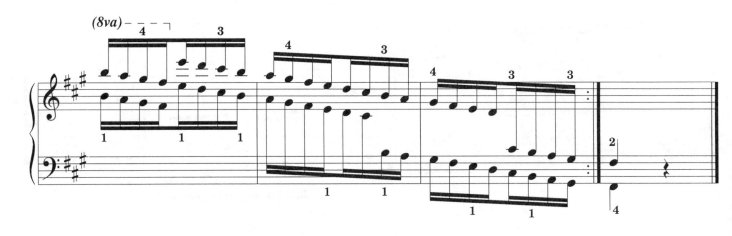

66

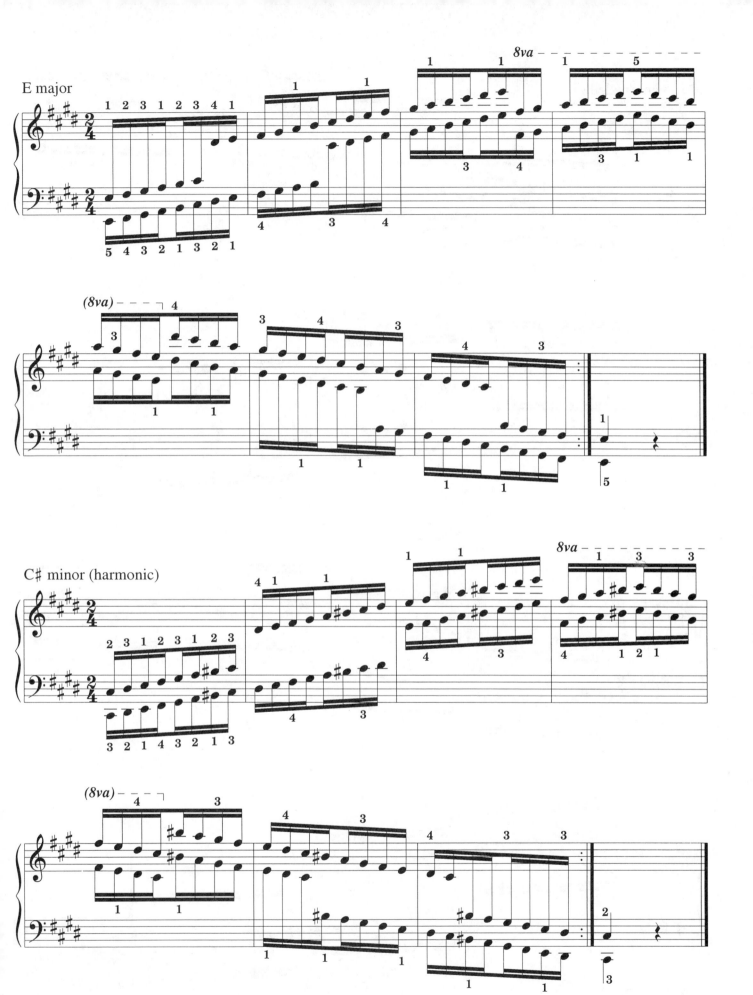

E major

C# minor (harmonic)

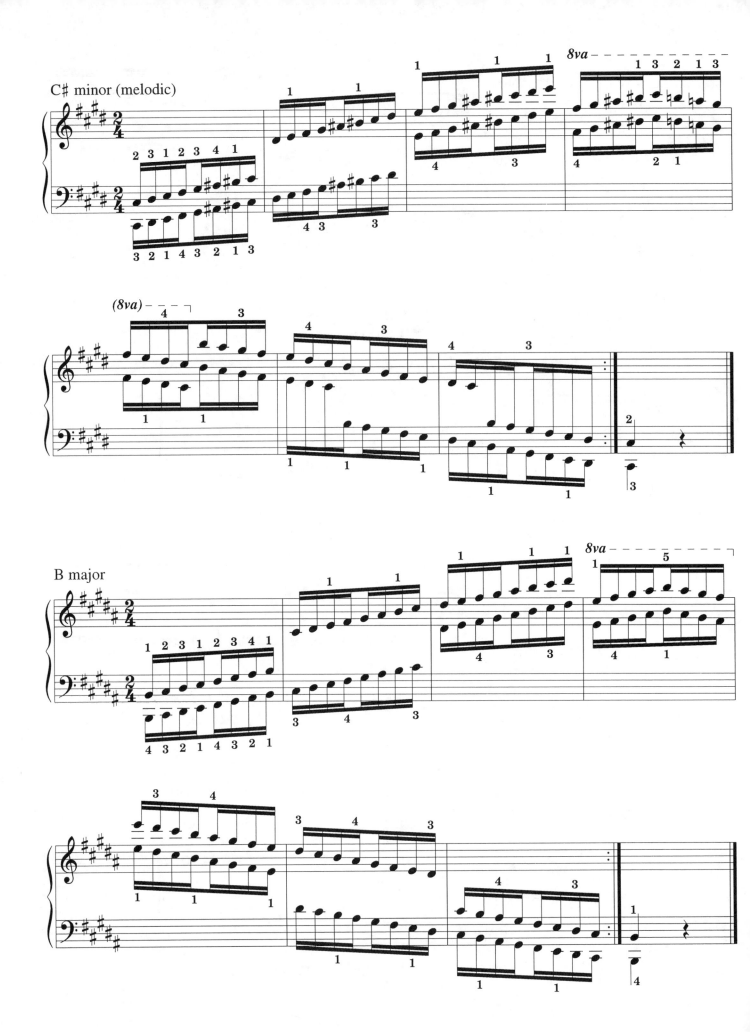

C# minor (melodic)

B major

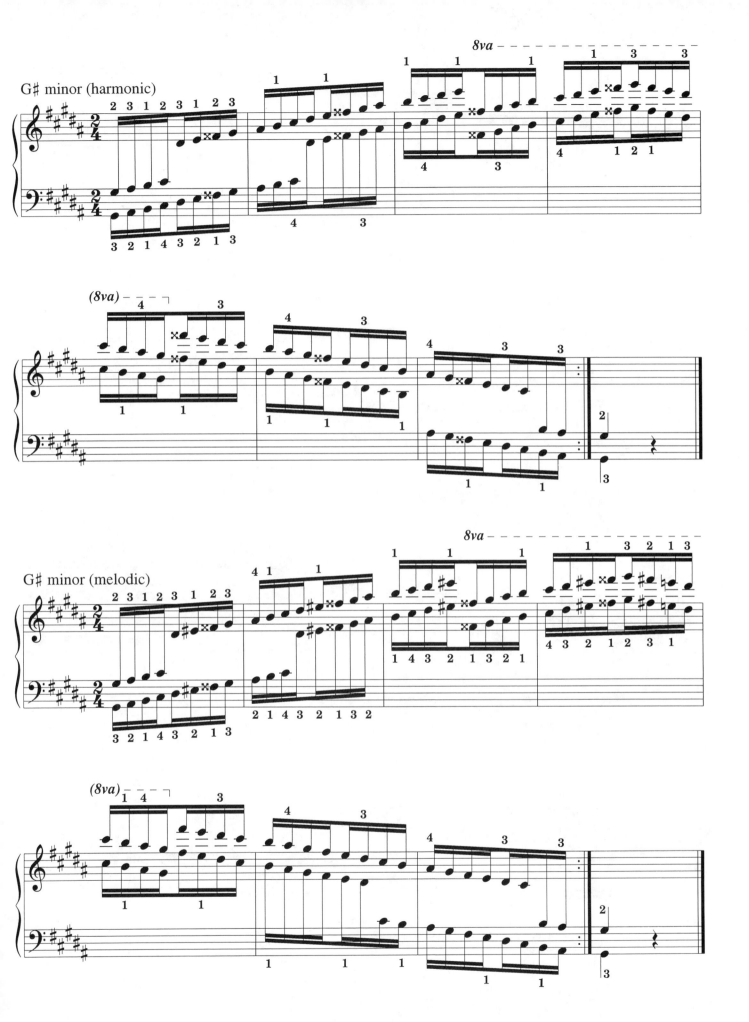

G# minor (harmonic)

G# minor (melodic)

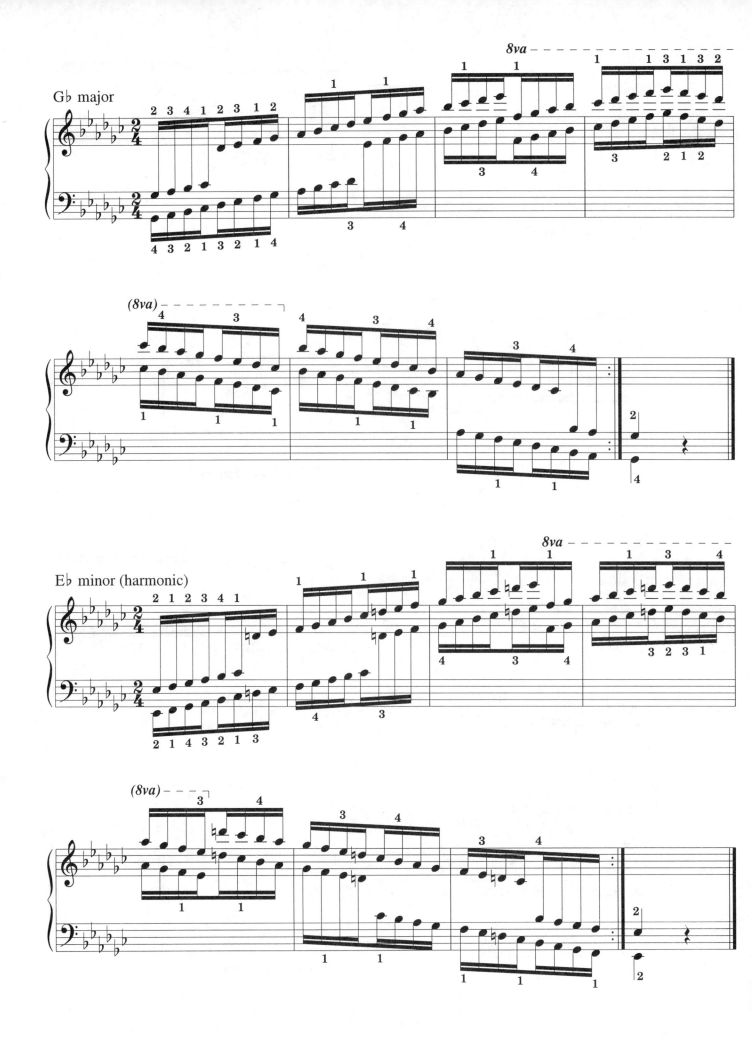

Gb major

Eb minor (harmonic)

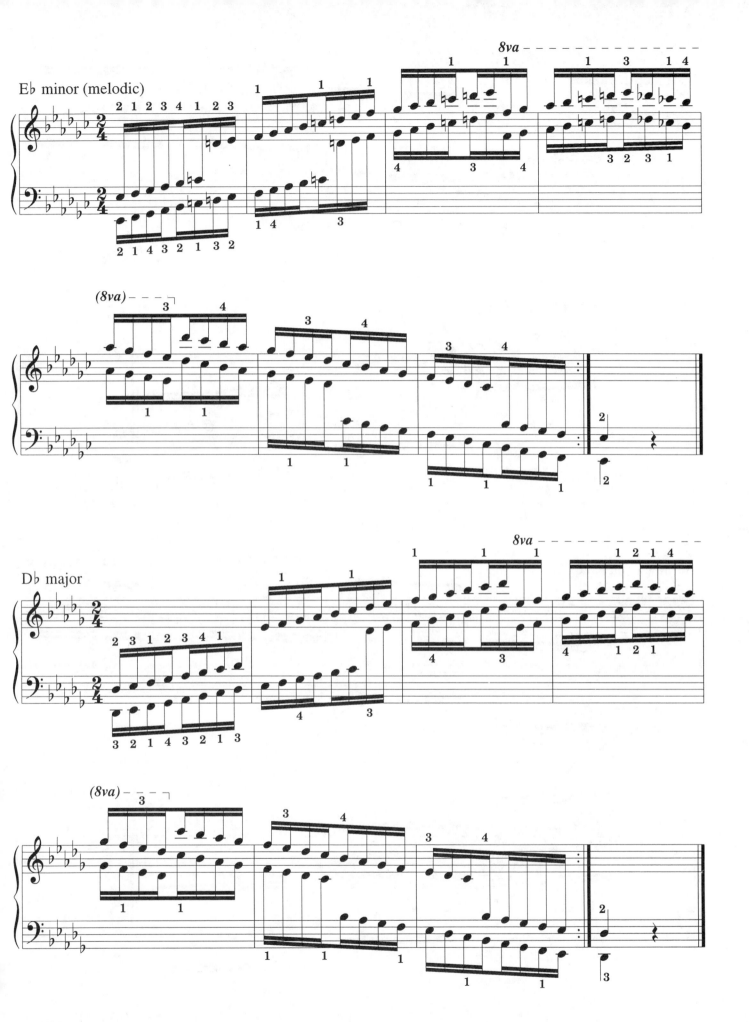

Eb minor (melodic)

Db major

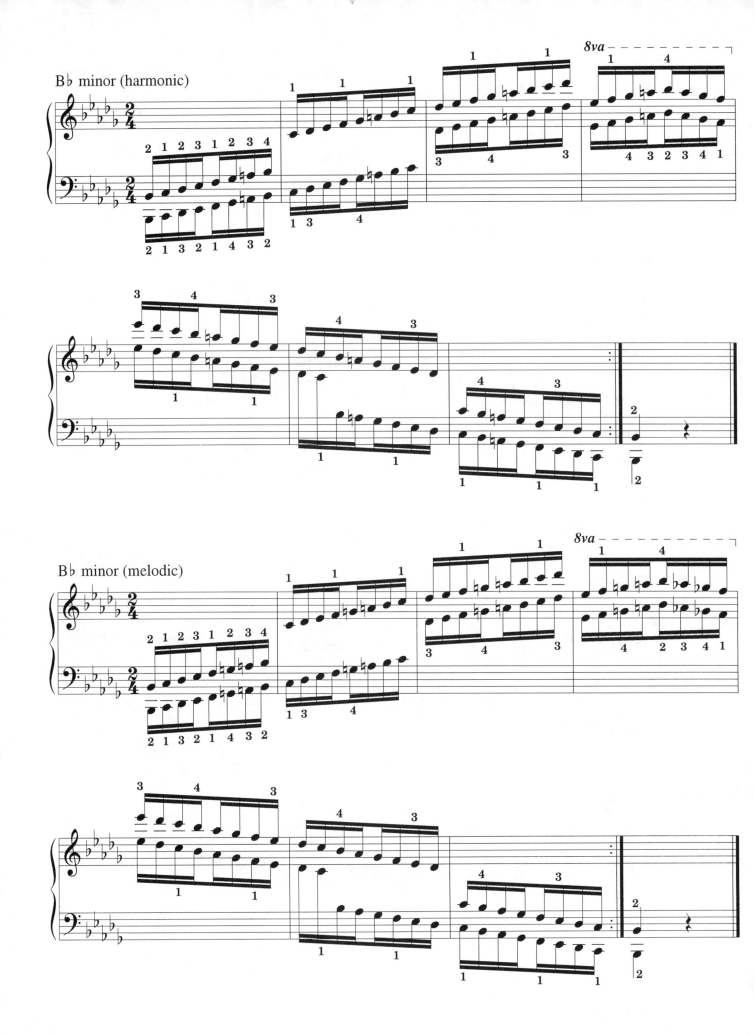

B♭ minor (harmonic)

B♭ minor (melodic)

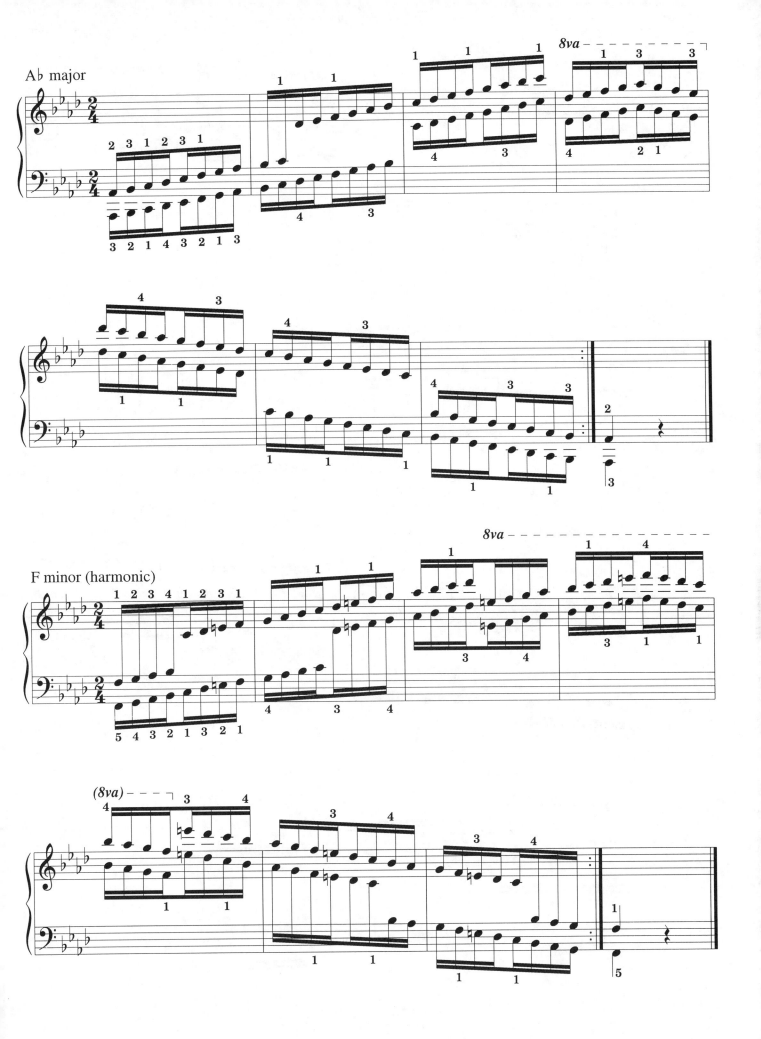

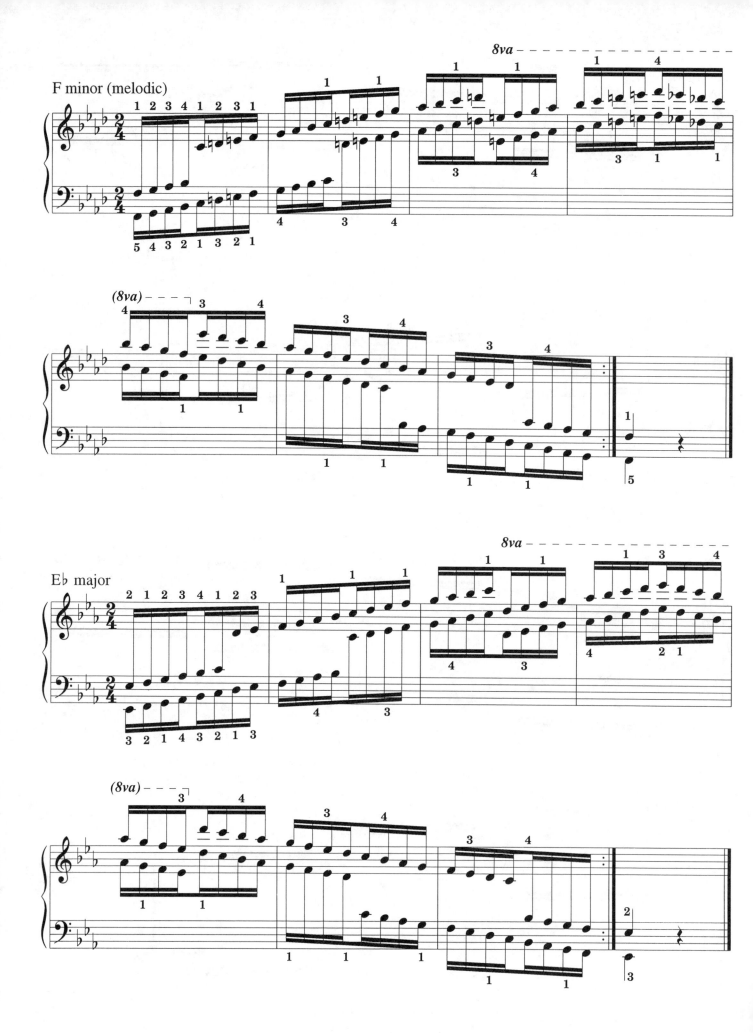

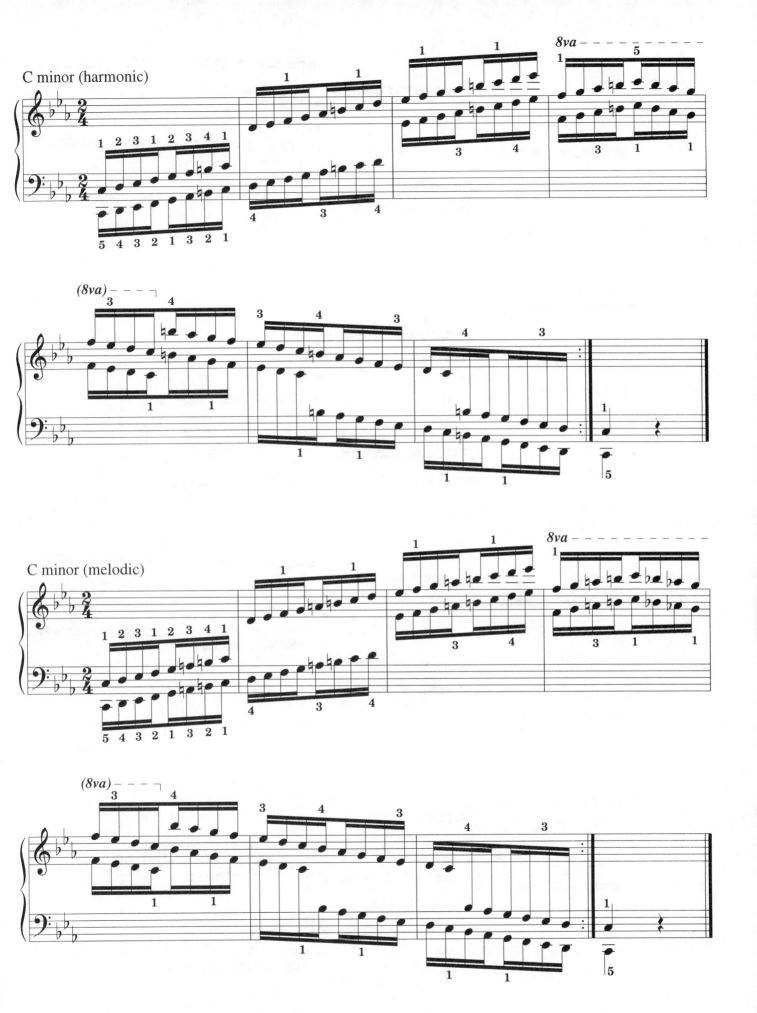

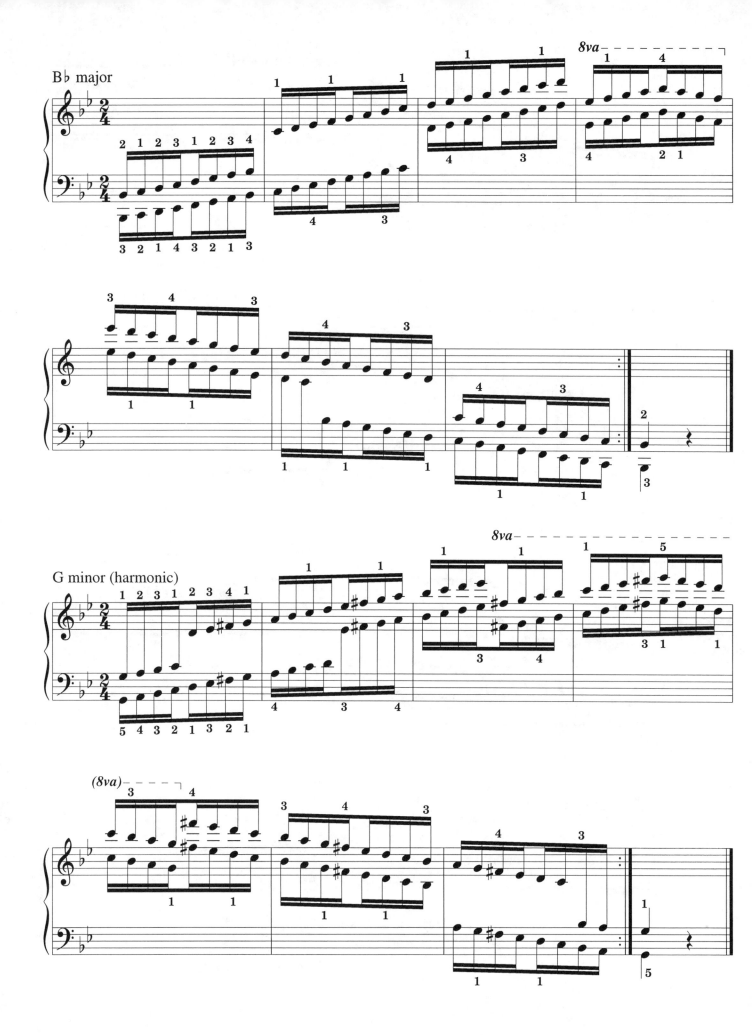

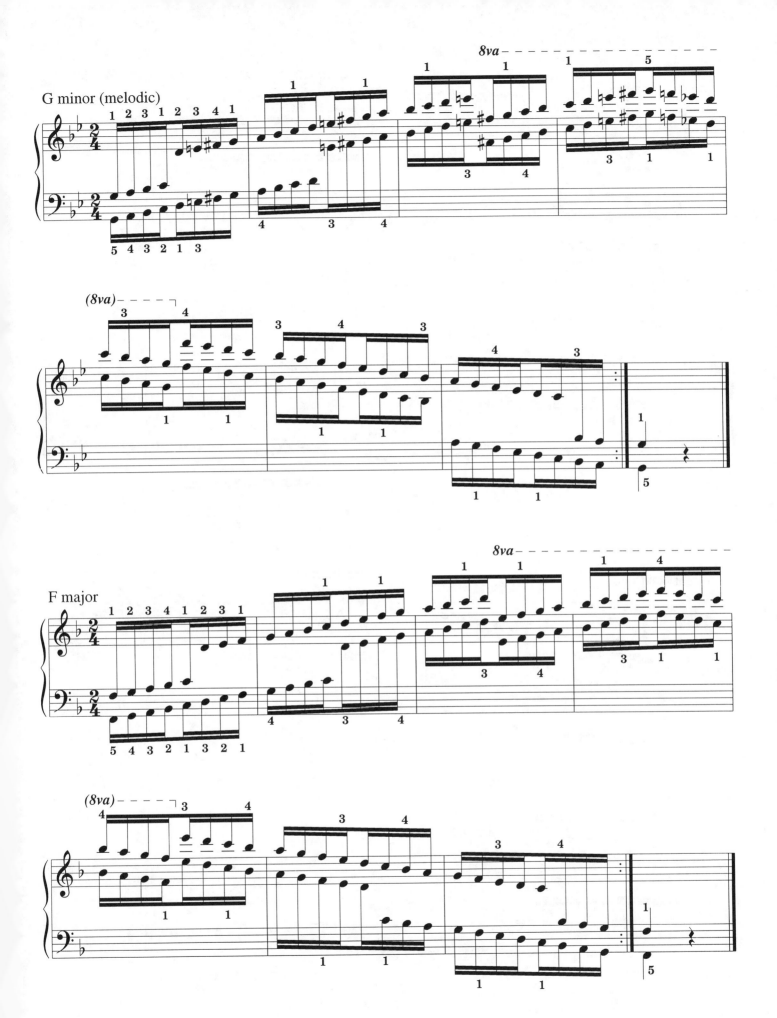

G minor (melodic)

F major

77

D minor (harmonic)

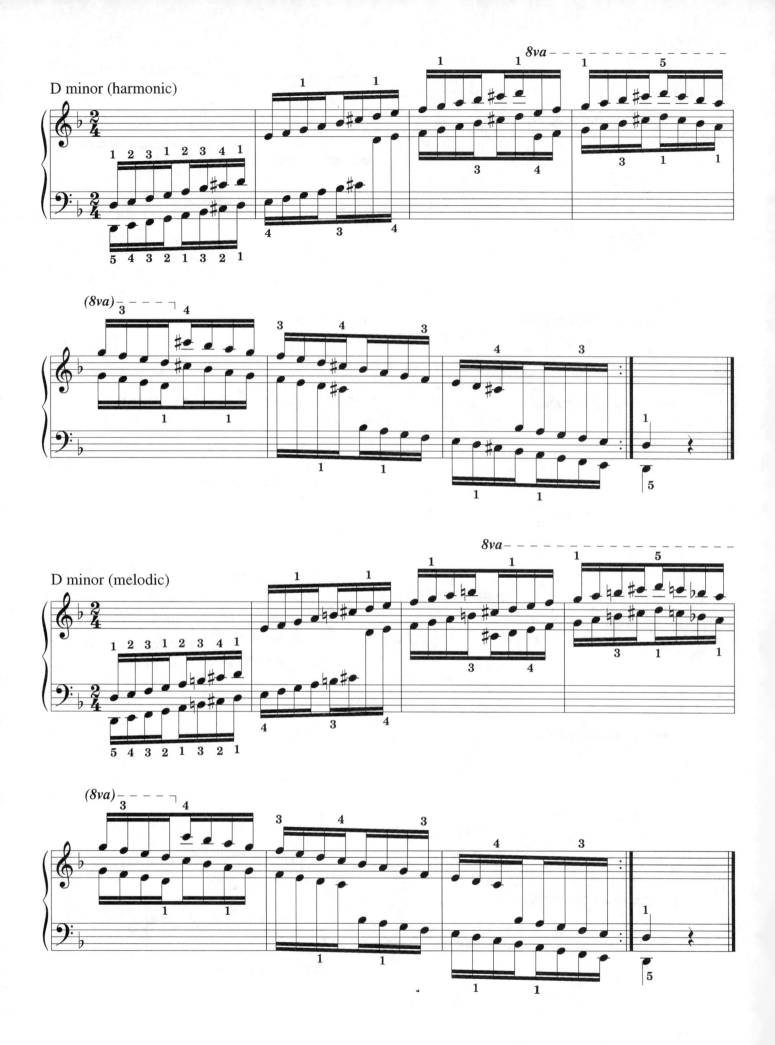

D minor (melodic)

SCALE CANONS

William Mason was the author of *Touch and Technic*. He studied in Europe with Franz Liszt. William Mason was the originator of using scale canon patterns. He taught that the great value of the Canon for scale practice was found in the individuality it gave to each hand. William was the son of the great Lowell Mason.

William Mason

Exercise 20

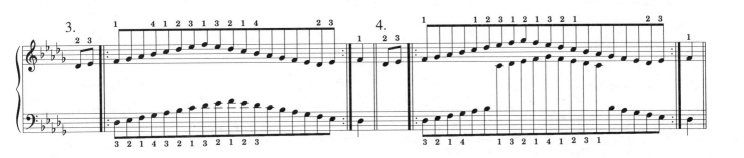

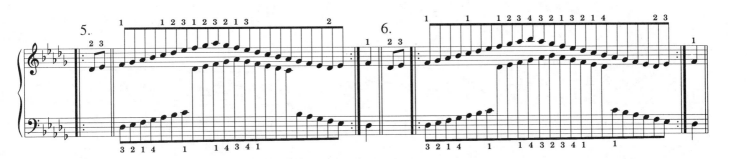

79

PATTERN CANON WITH BOTH TURNING POINTS MOVABLE

William Mason

In ascending the up scales are an octave, and the down scales seven, in descending this is reversed, the descents being an octave and the ascents seven degrees.

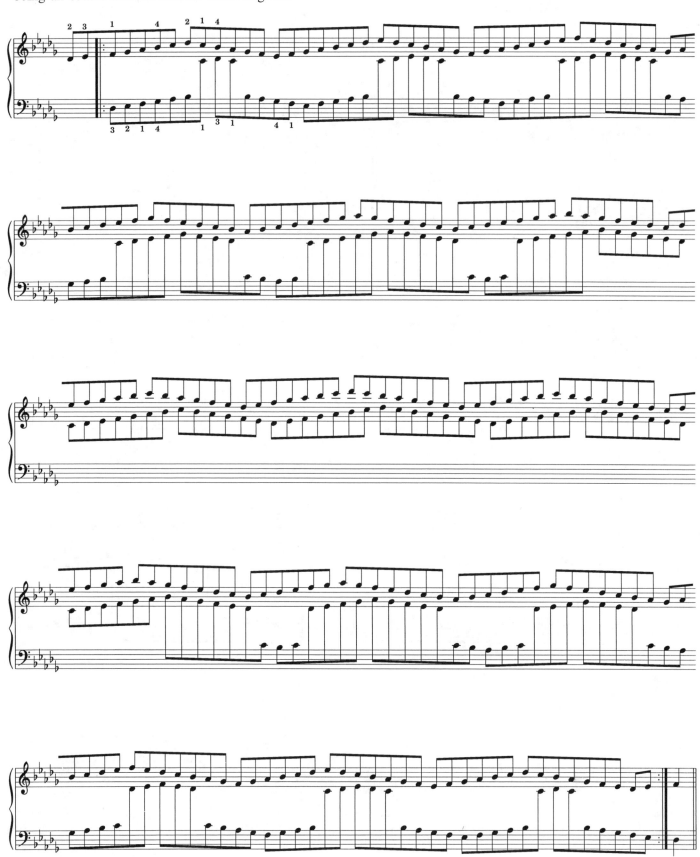

80

C Minor Scale Canon

William Mason

(1) Compass of one Octave

(2) Through Nine tones.

(3) Compass of a Tenth.

(4) Compass of a Eleventh.

(5) Compass of a Twelfth.

(6) Compass of a Thirteenth

(7) Compass of a Fourteenth.

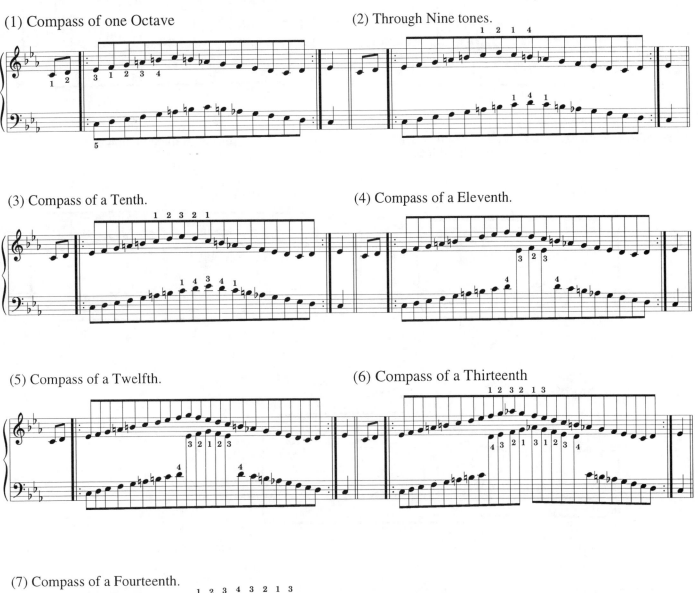

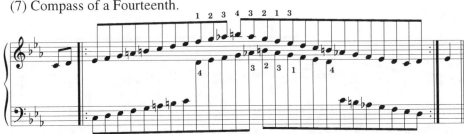

(8) Compass of Two octaves. Precisely the same as No. 1 extended an octave.
(9) Compass of Three octaves.

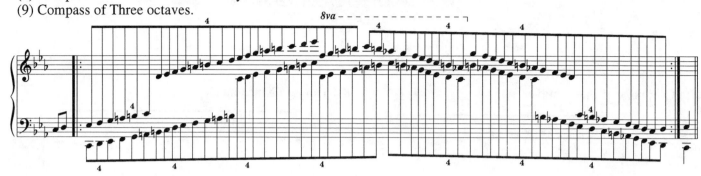

The following are examples, or patterns, in which the left hand leads. All the distances must be practiced in this form as well as in the form where the right hand leads.

(10) Compass of One octave.   (11) Turning on the Sixth above.

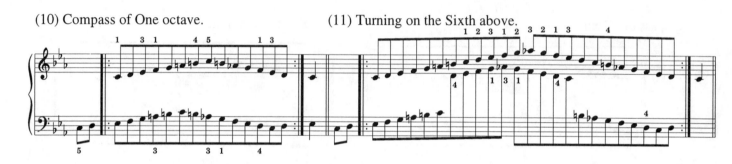

(12) Turning on the Seventh.

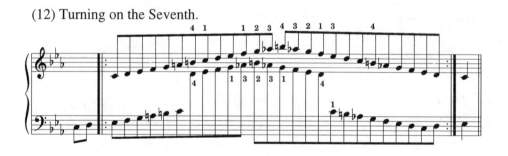

(13) Pattern extending through Four octaves.

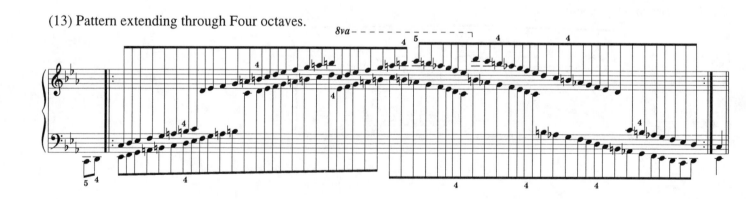

Extended Arpeggios in all Major and Minor Keys

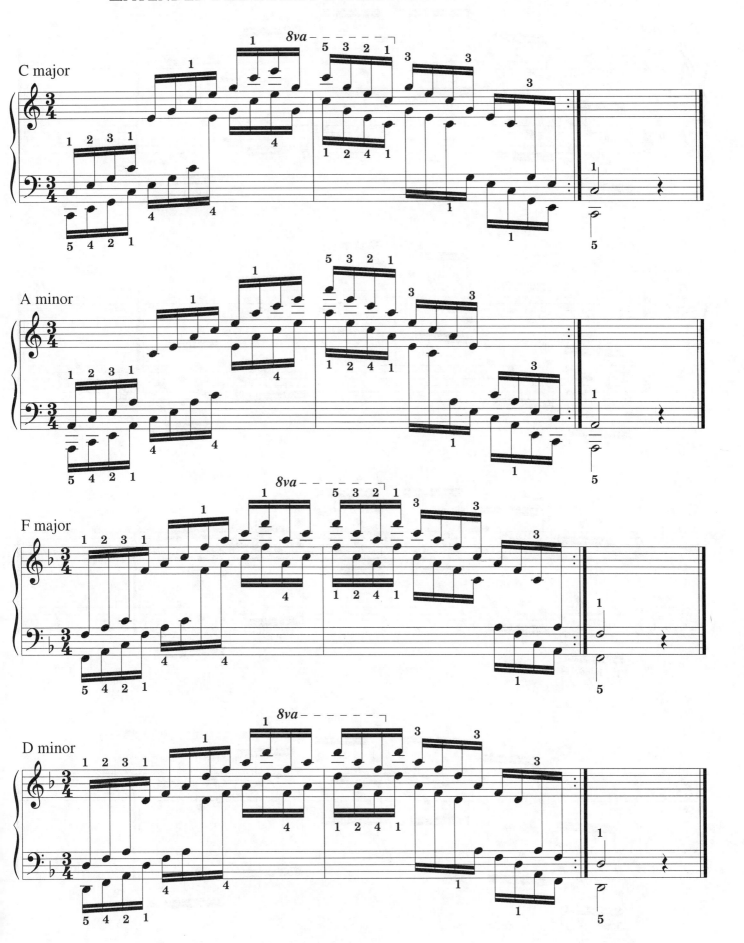

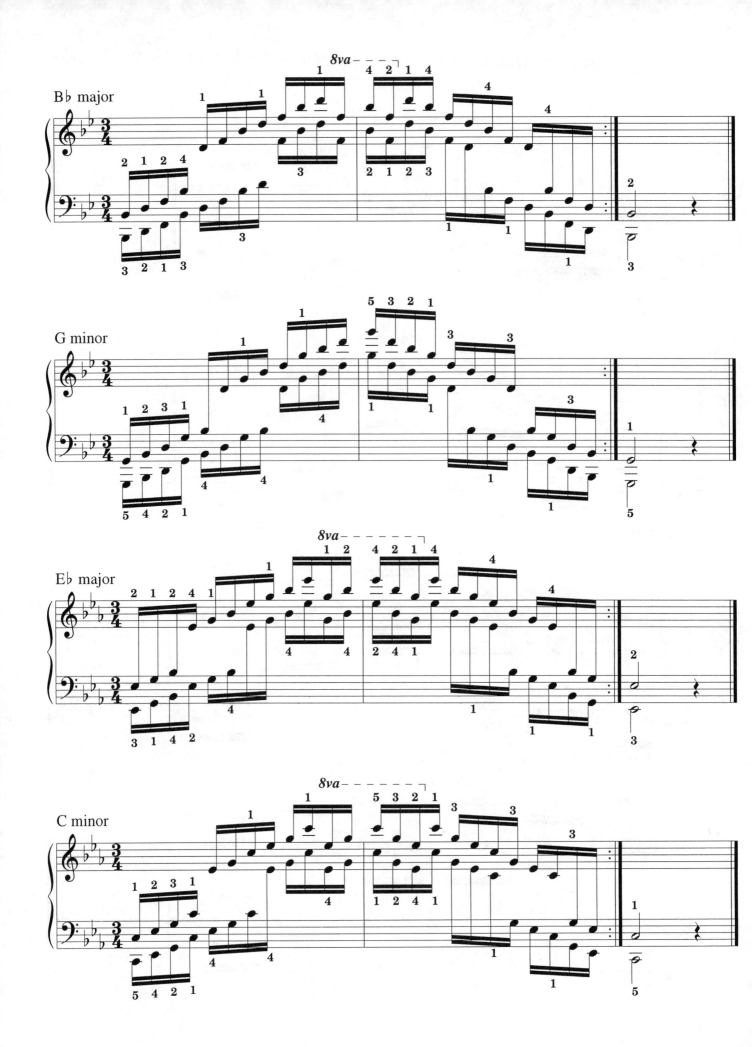

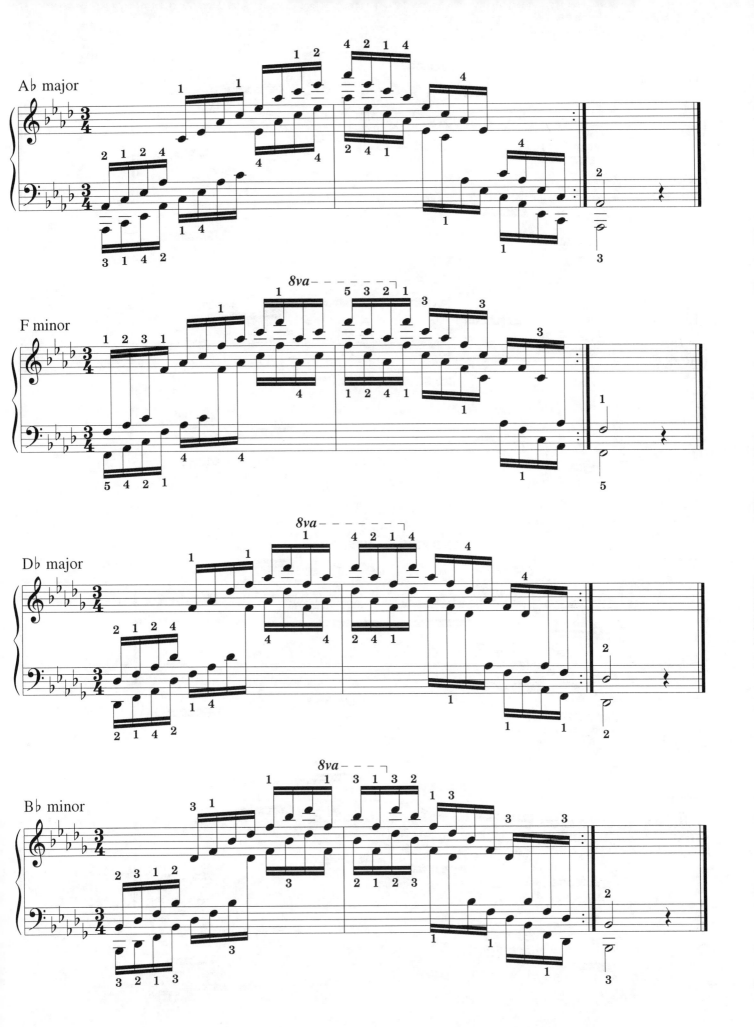

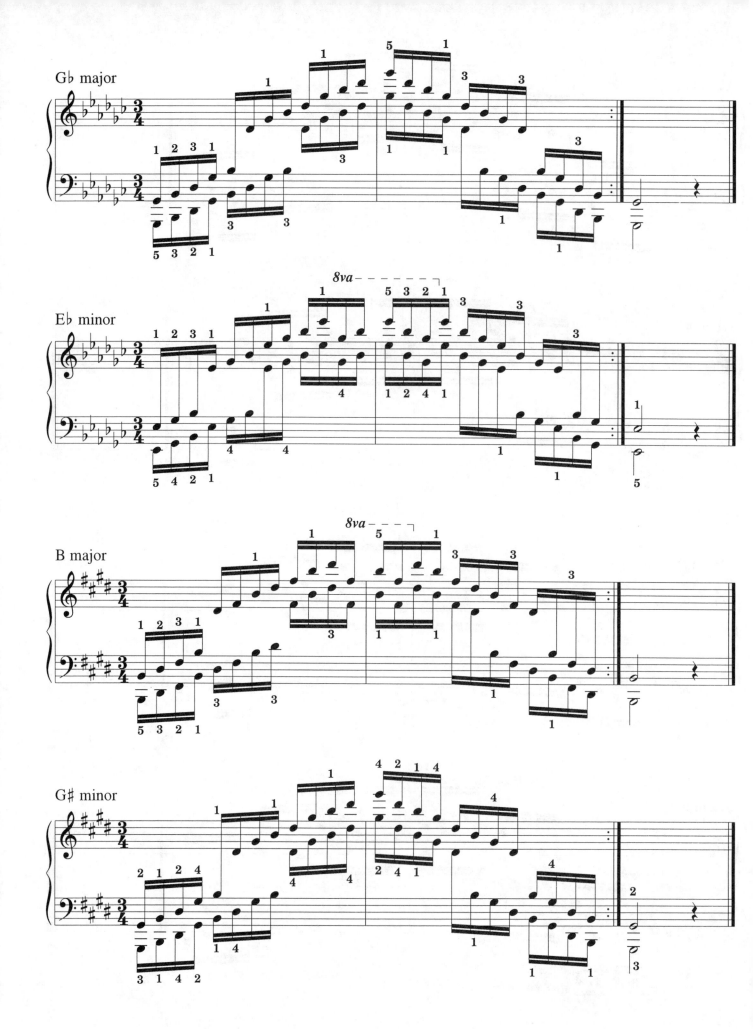

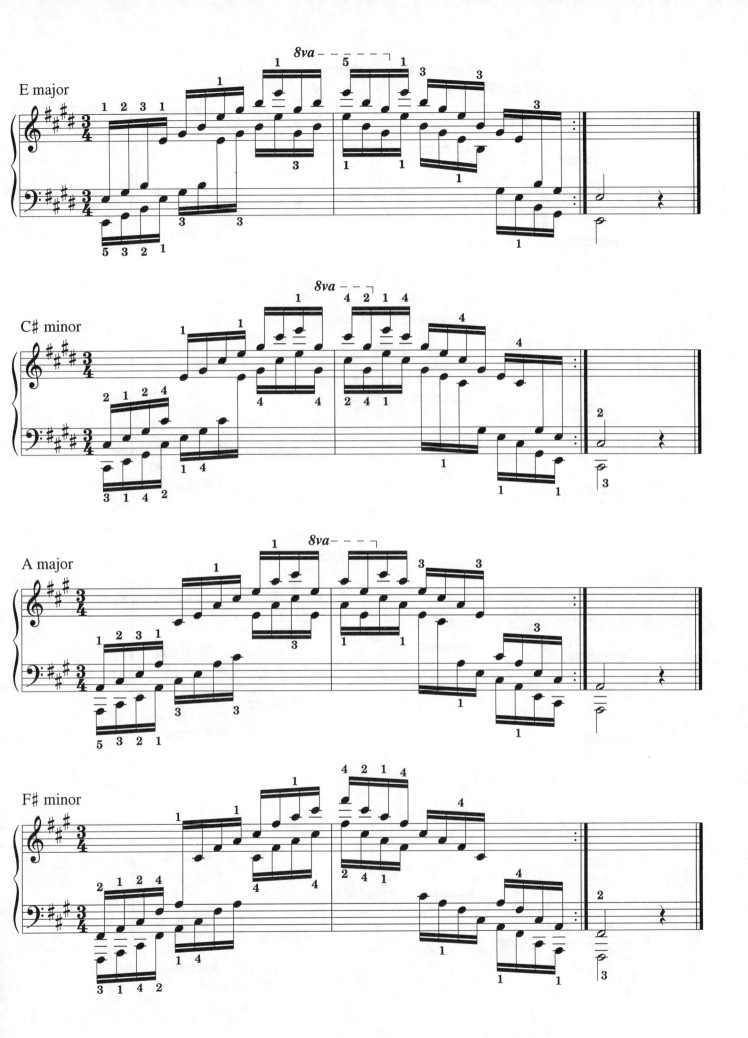

87

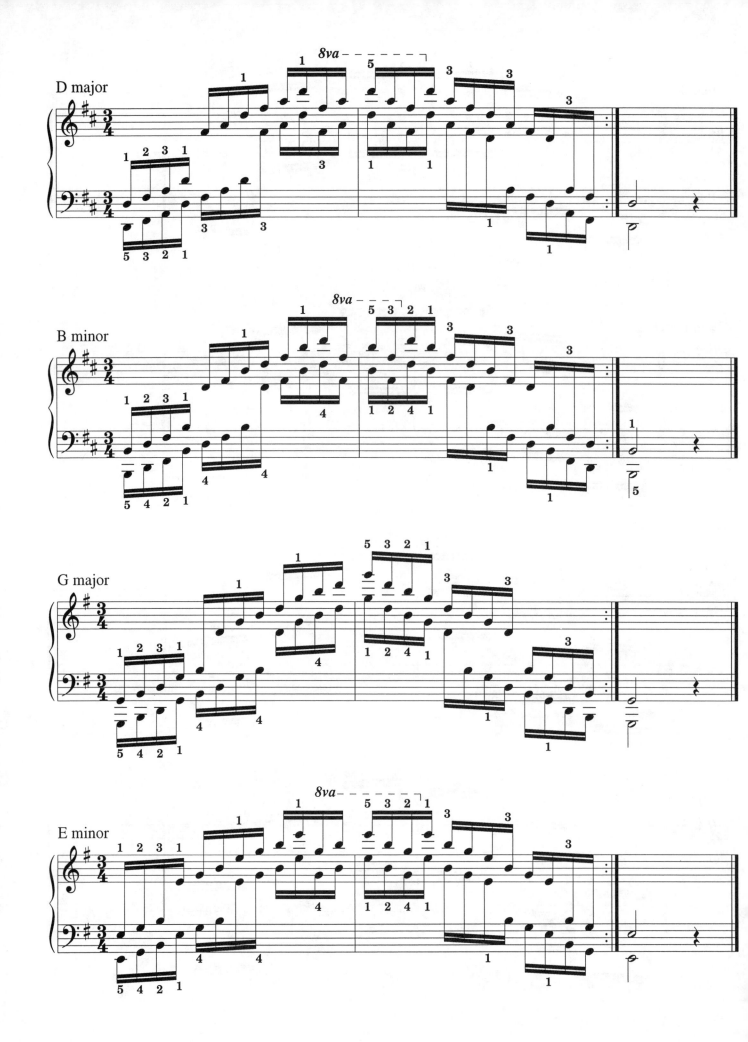

EXTENDED ARPEGGIOS IN DOMINANT SEVENTH CHORDS

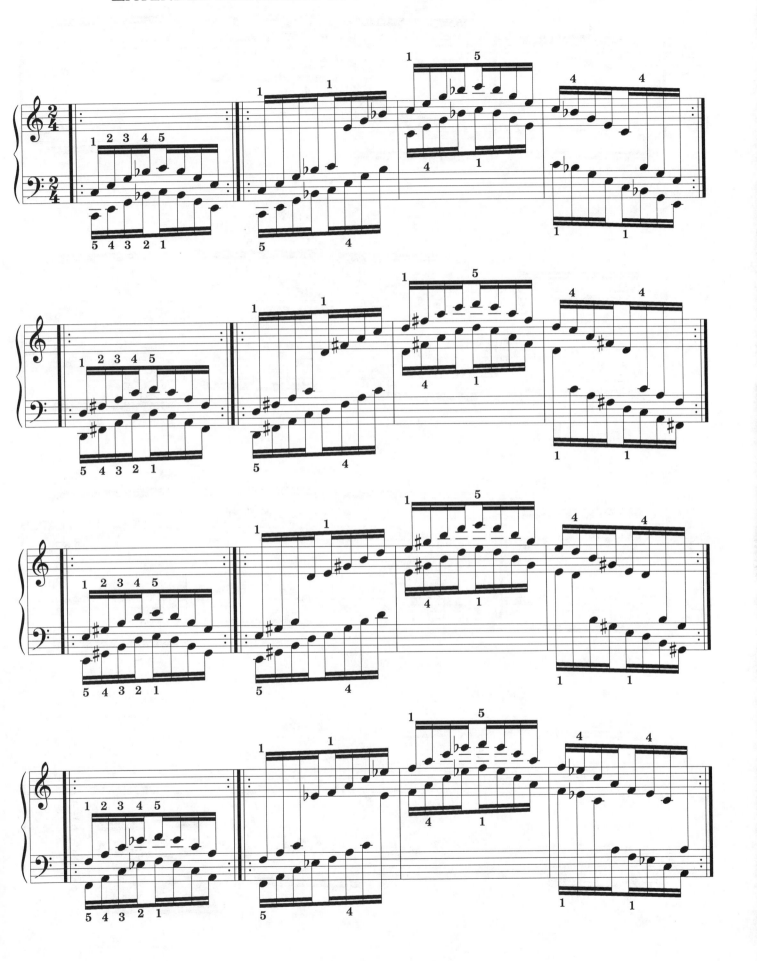

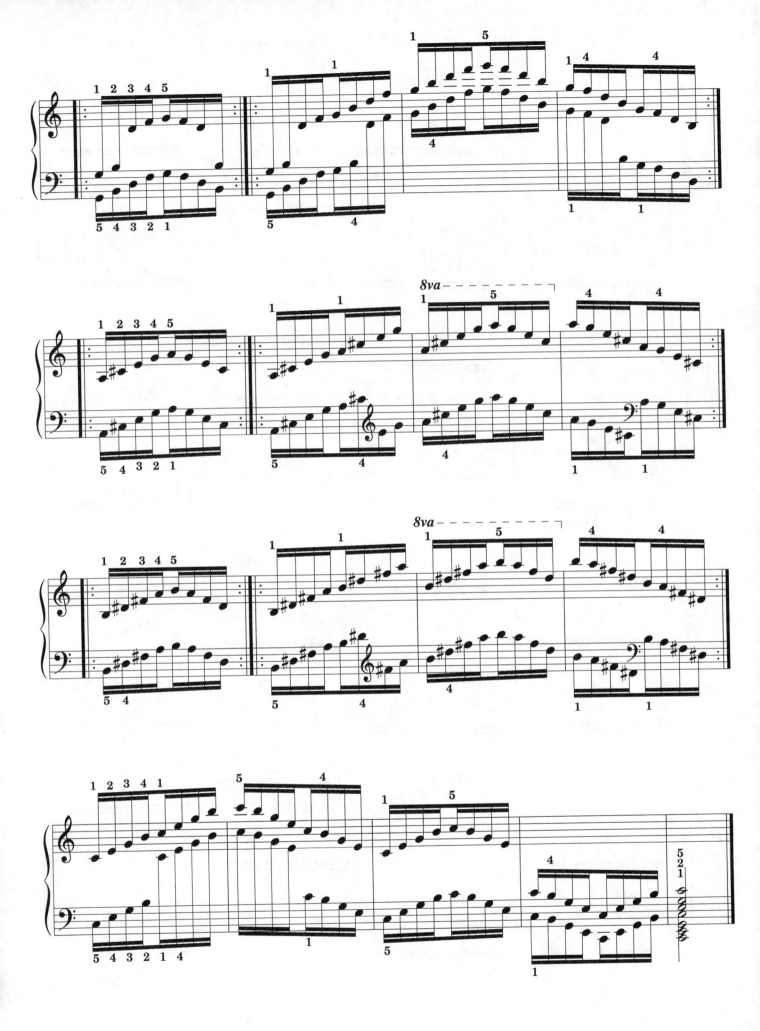

School of Velocity Op. 299, No. 1
Two Octave Scale Study for the Right Hand

Carl Czerny

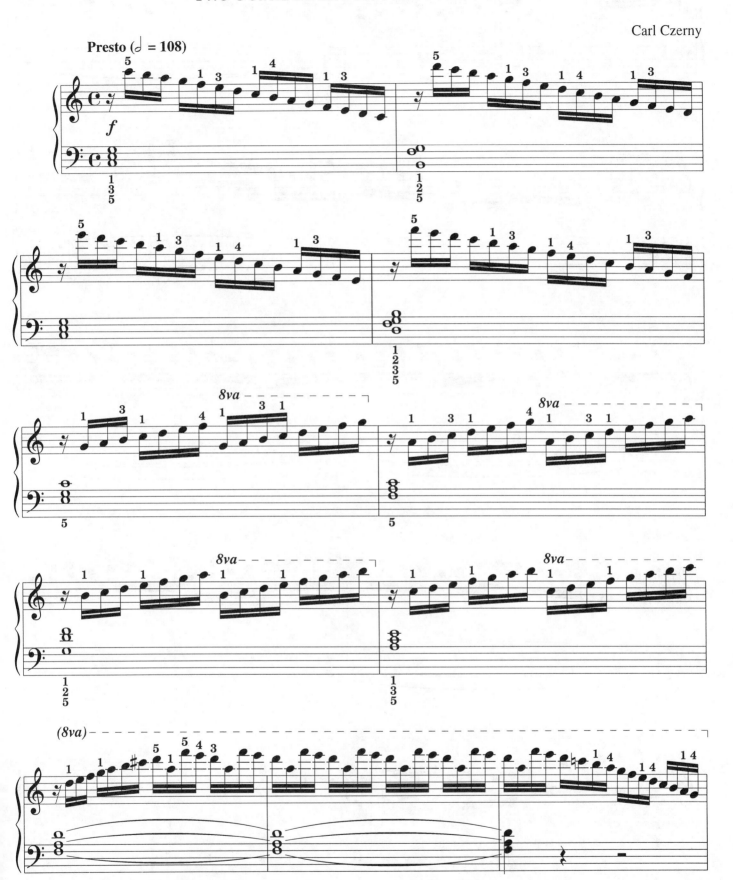

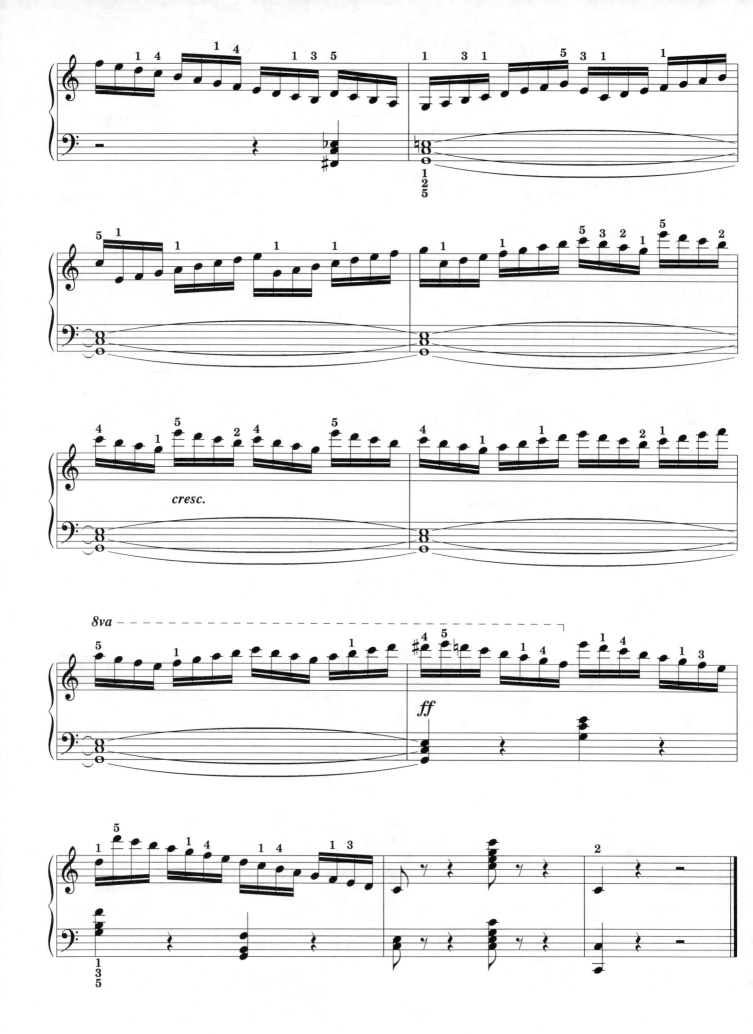

Op. 299, No. 2
Two Octave Scale Study for the Left hand

Carl Czerny

Op. 299, No. 3

ARPEGGIO EXERCISE

Carl Czerny

96

THE TURN EXERCISE
OP. 299, No. 4

Carl Czerny

cresc.

8va - - - - - - - - - - - - - - - - - -

f

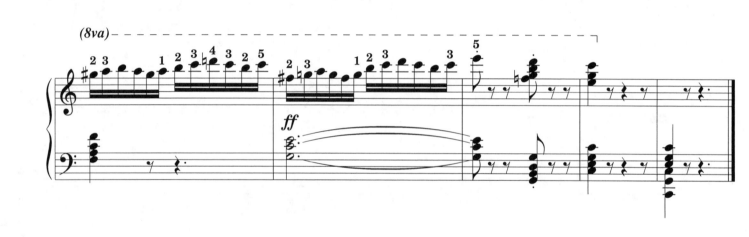

(8va) - - - - - - - - - - - - - - - - - -

ff

FINGER WARM-UP
Op. 299, No. 20

Carl Czerny

A Canon Exercise
from Gradus ad Parnassum No. 14

Muzio Clementi

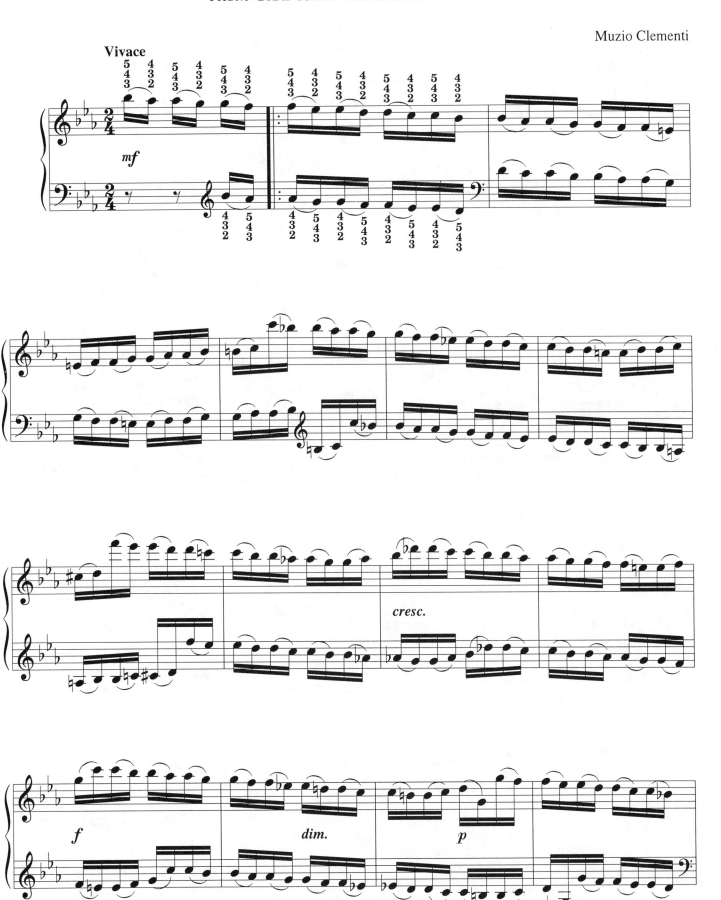

Etùde
Op. 10, No. 1

F. Chopin

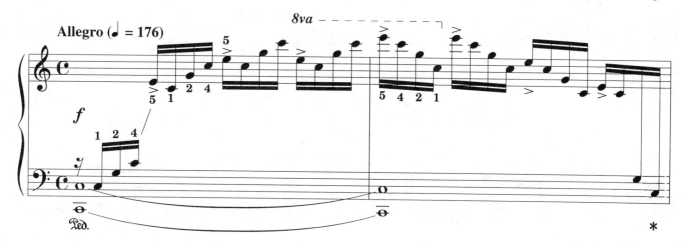

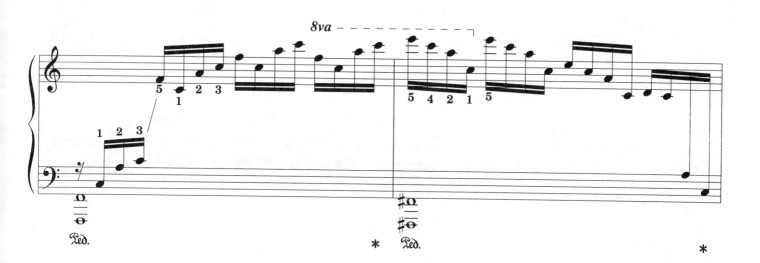

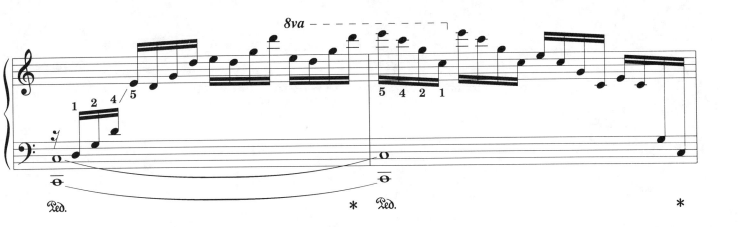

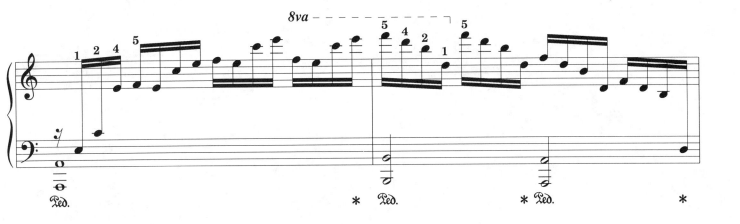

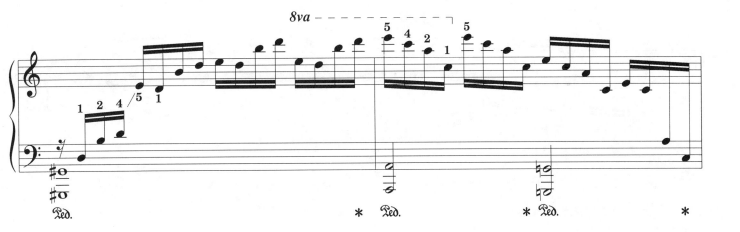

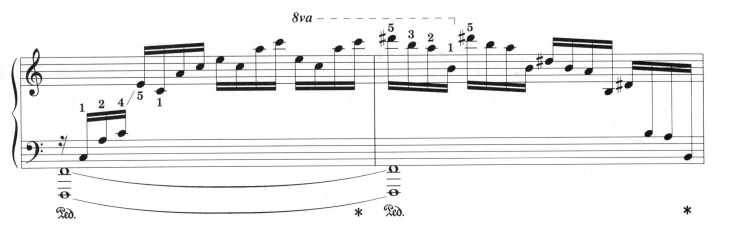

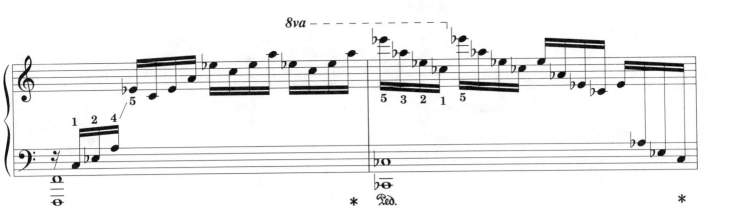

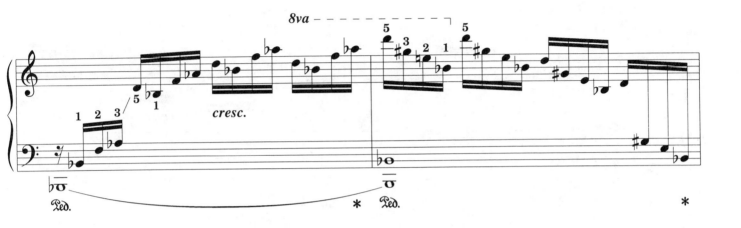

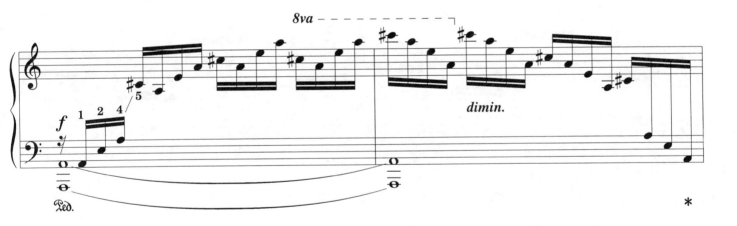

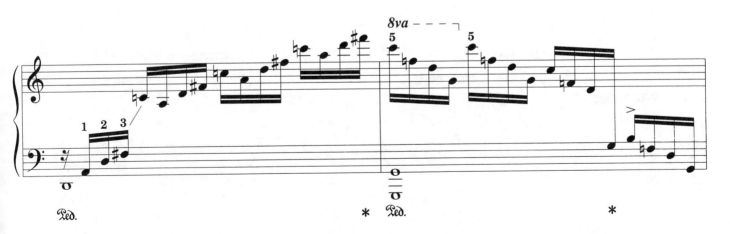

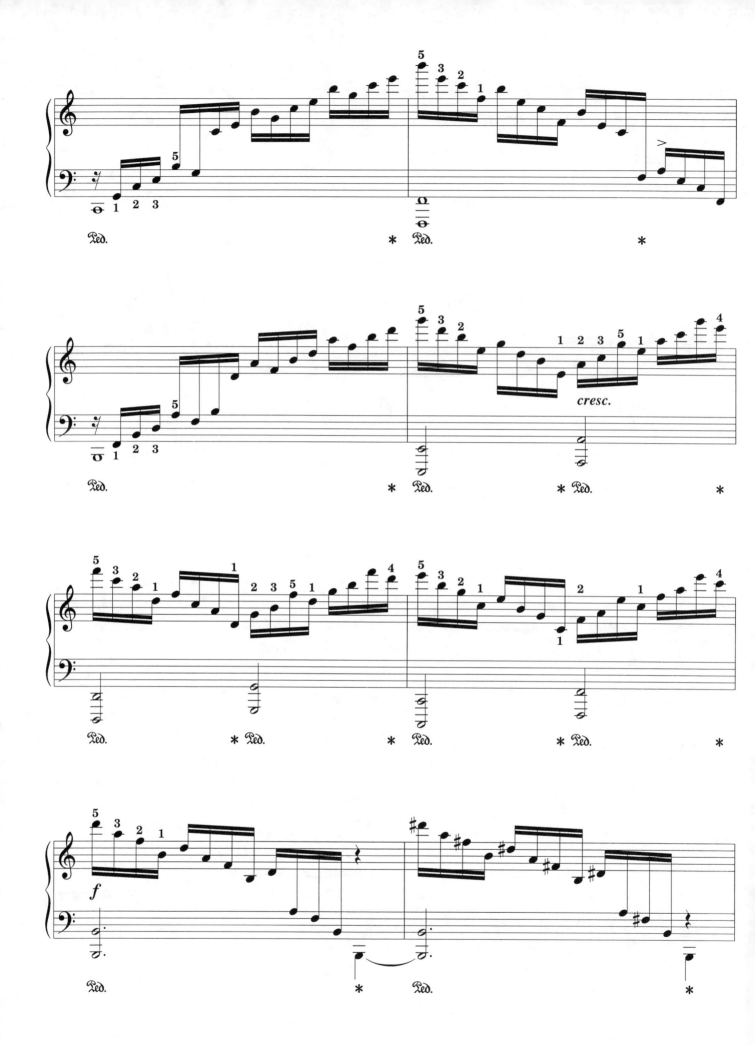

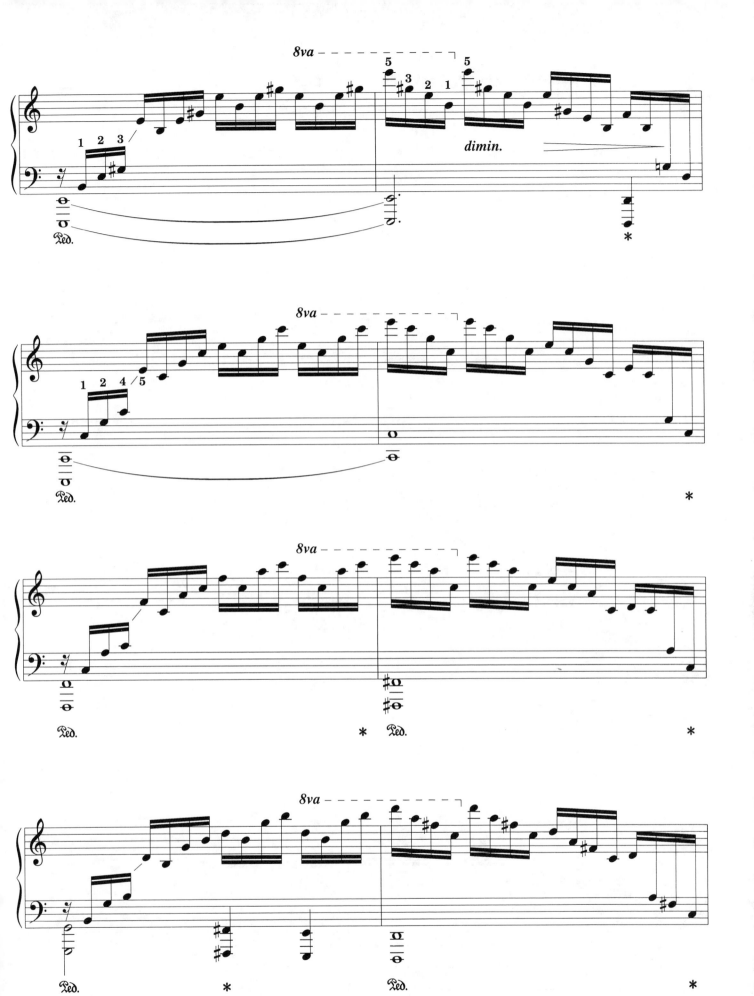

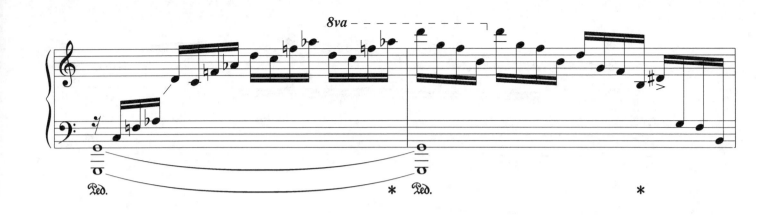

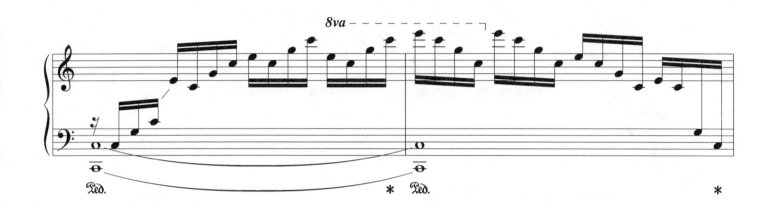

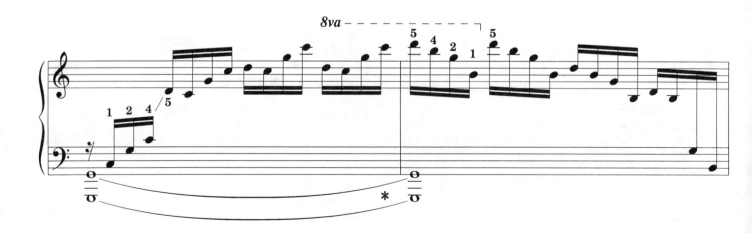

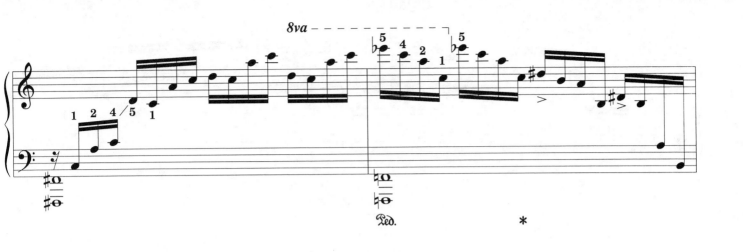

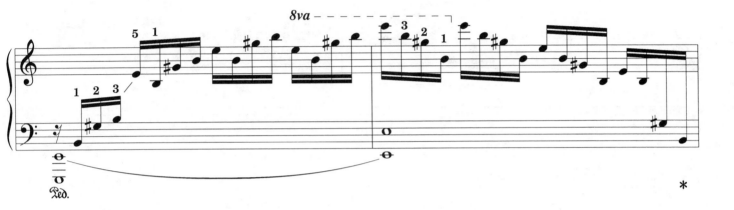

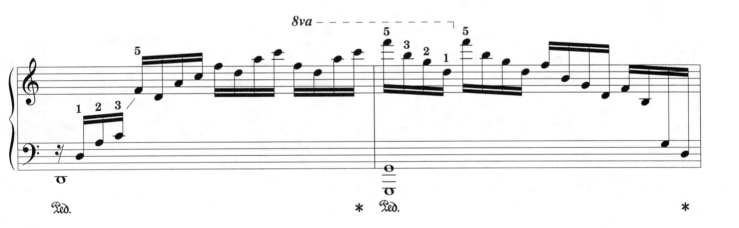

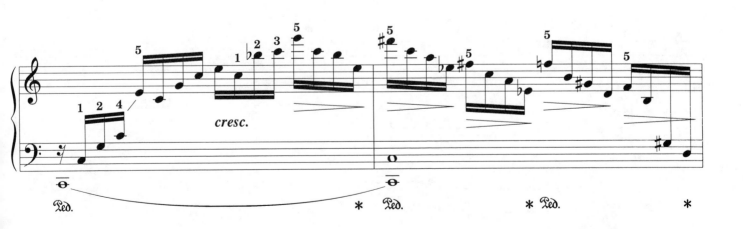

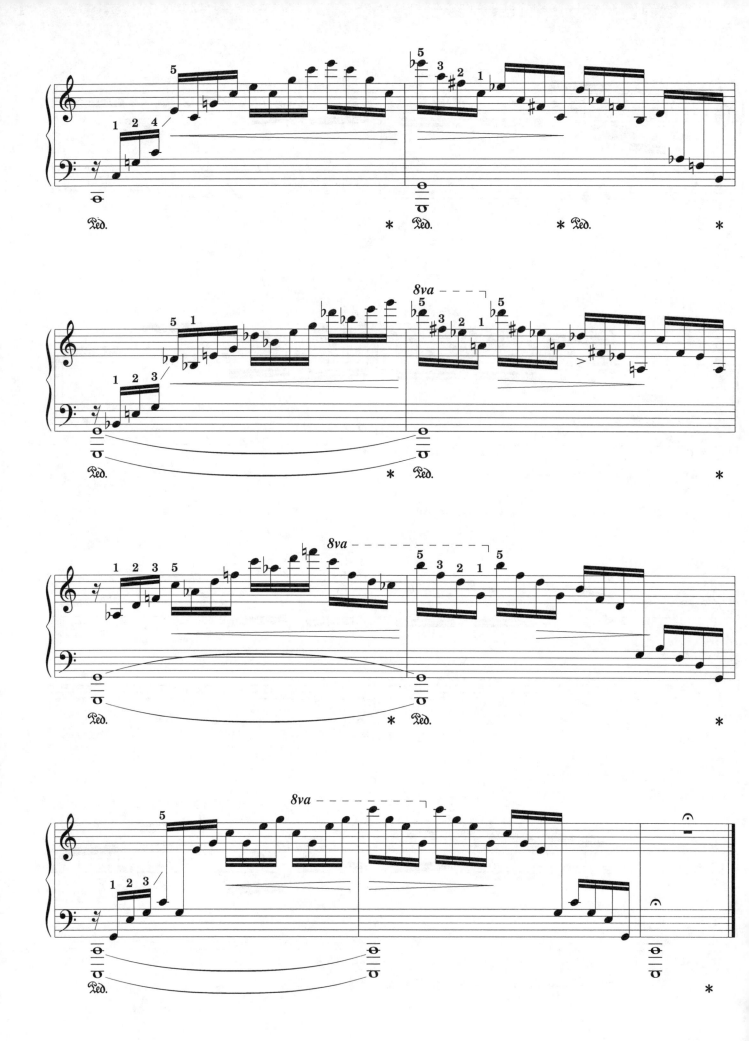

114

Two Against Three Exercises
(Preliminary)

Two against two.

Two against three.

Two Exercises from 51 Exercises

FOR THE PIANO

Johannes Brahms

2.

The Art of Finger-Dexterity
Op. 740, No. 1

C. Czerny

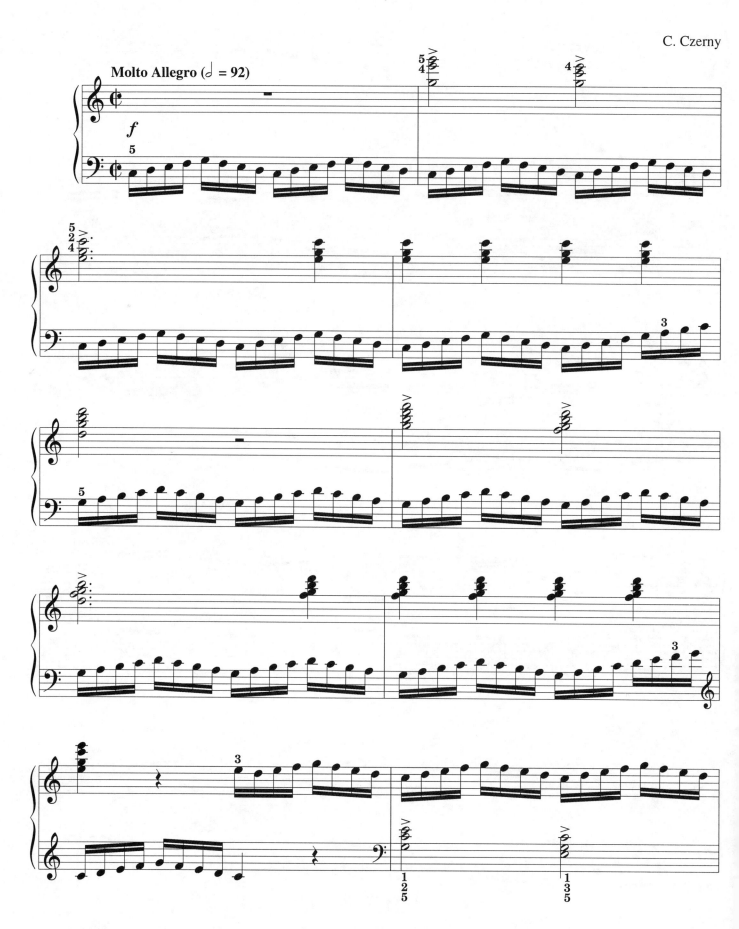

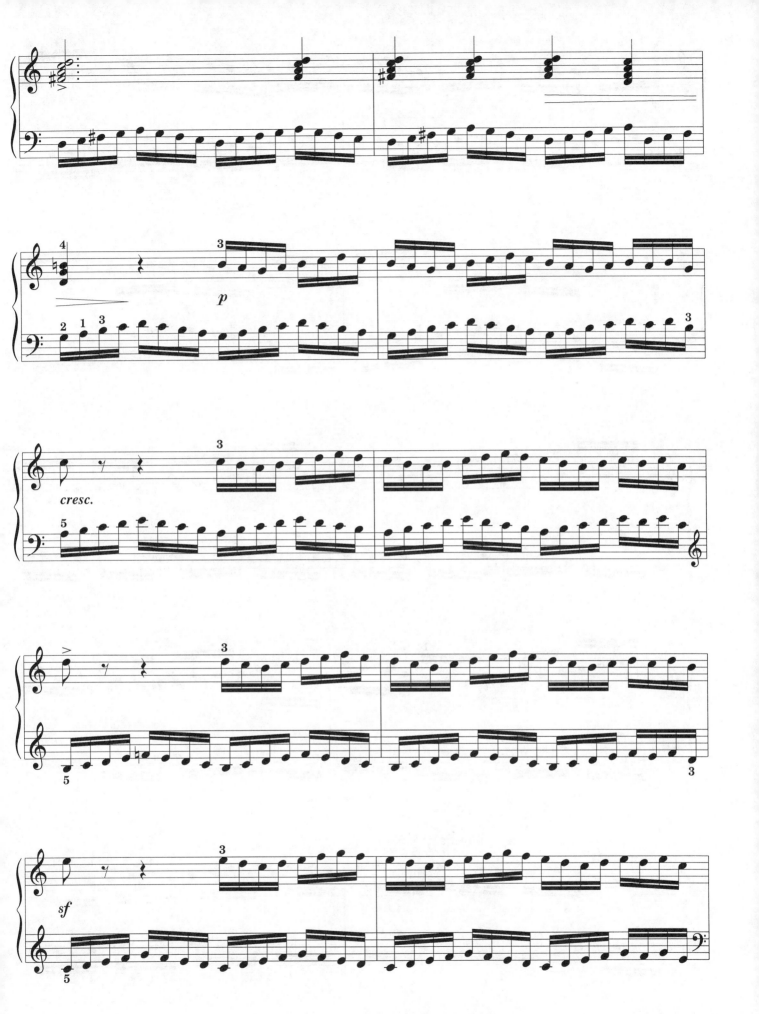

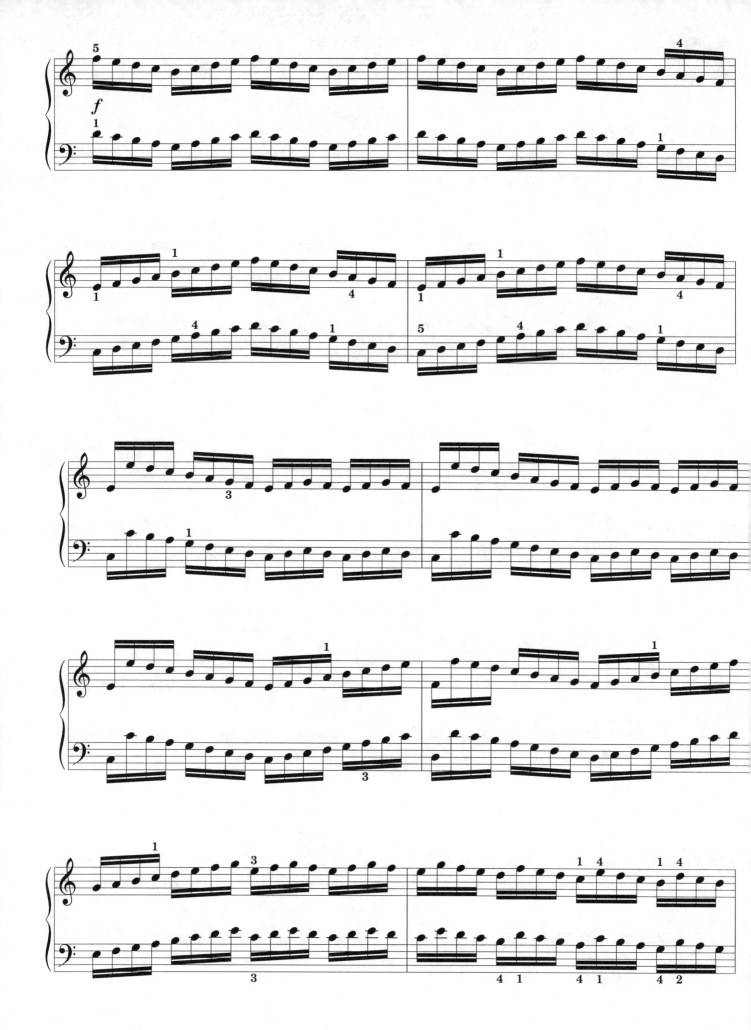

126

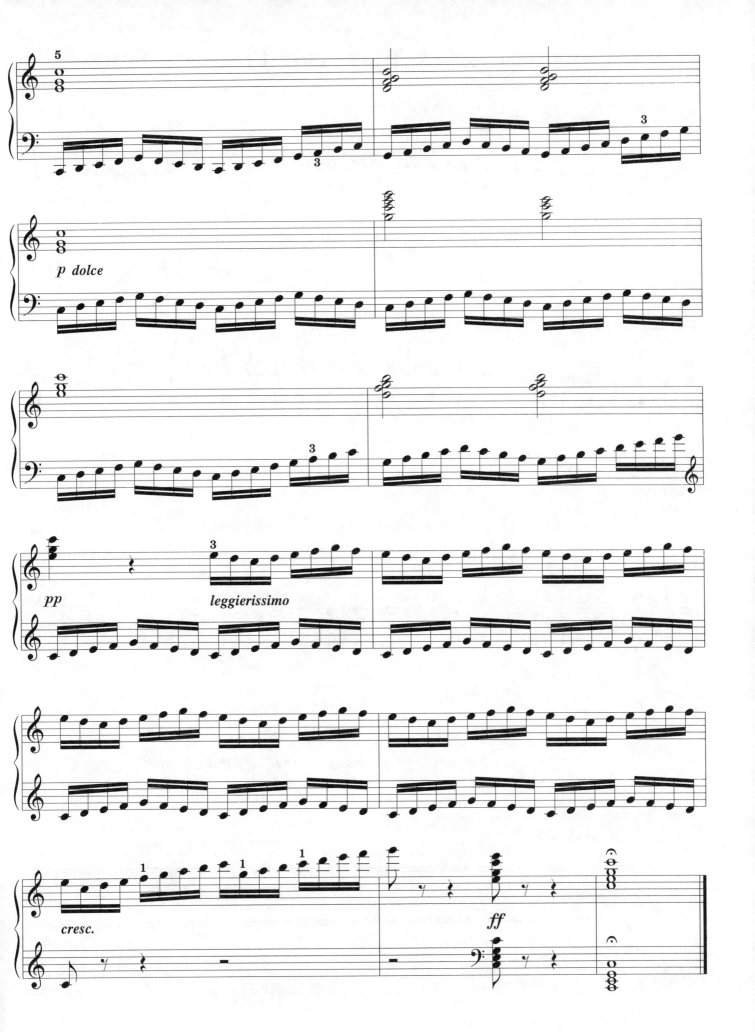

CHOPIN'S AND CZERNY'S FINGERINGS OF CHROMATIC SCALES

Fingering for Chromatic Scales (Czerny)

Fingering for Chromatic Major Thirds (Czerny)

Czerny's fingering for chromatic thirds has been universally accepted.

Fingering for Chromatic Minor Thirds (Czerny)

Chopin used the first finger on consecutive white keys, (E-F),(B-C)
Liszt, among many others, liked to write major chromatic thirds.

Liszt: Rhapsodie, No. 15, Cadenza

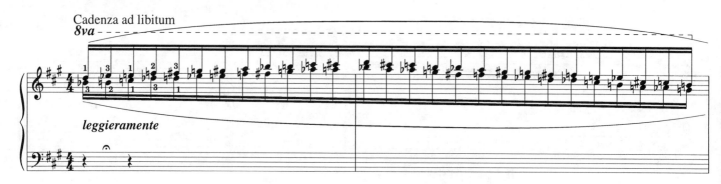

CHROMATIC SCALES
AT AN OCTAVE

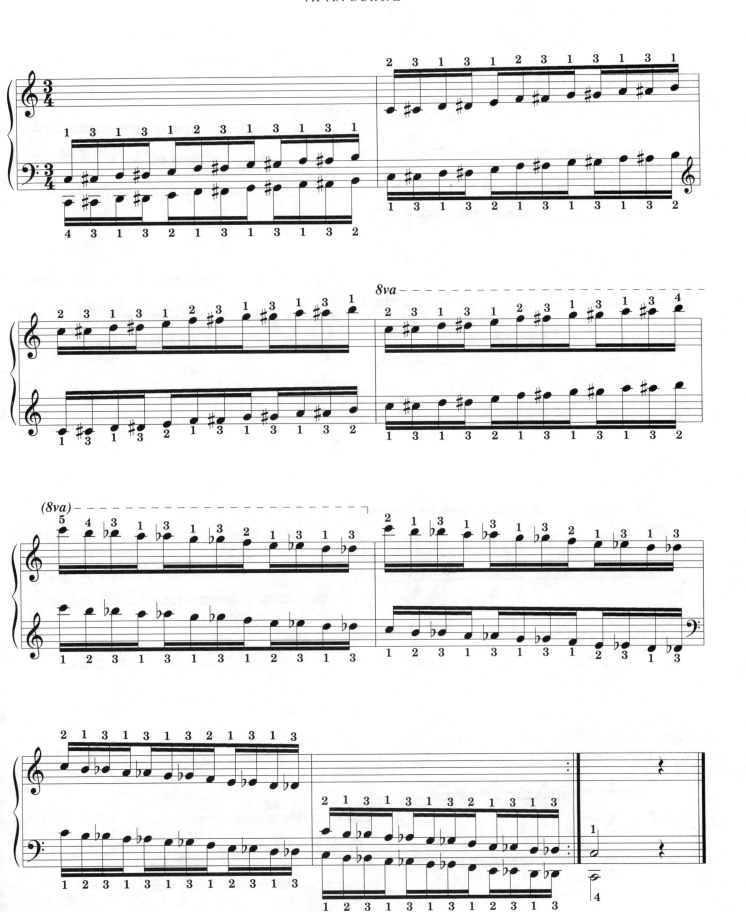

CHROMATIC SCALES
AT A MINOR THIRD

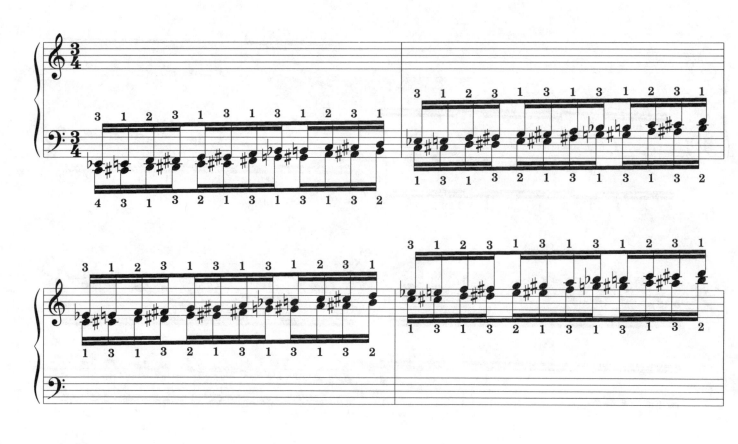

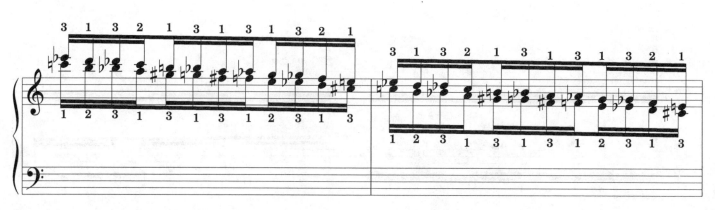

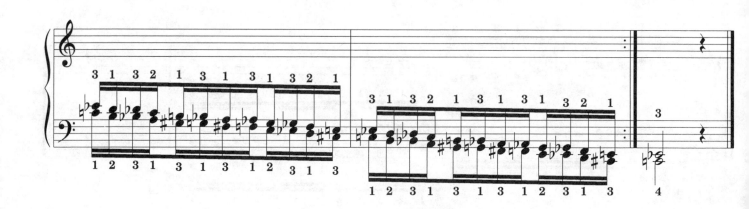

CHROMATIC SCALES
AT A MAJOR SIXTH

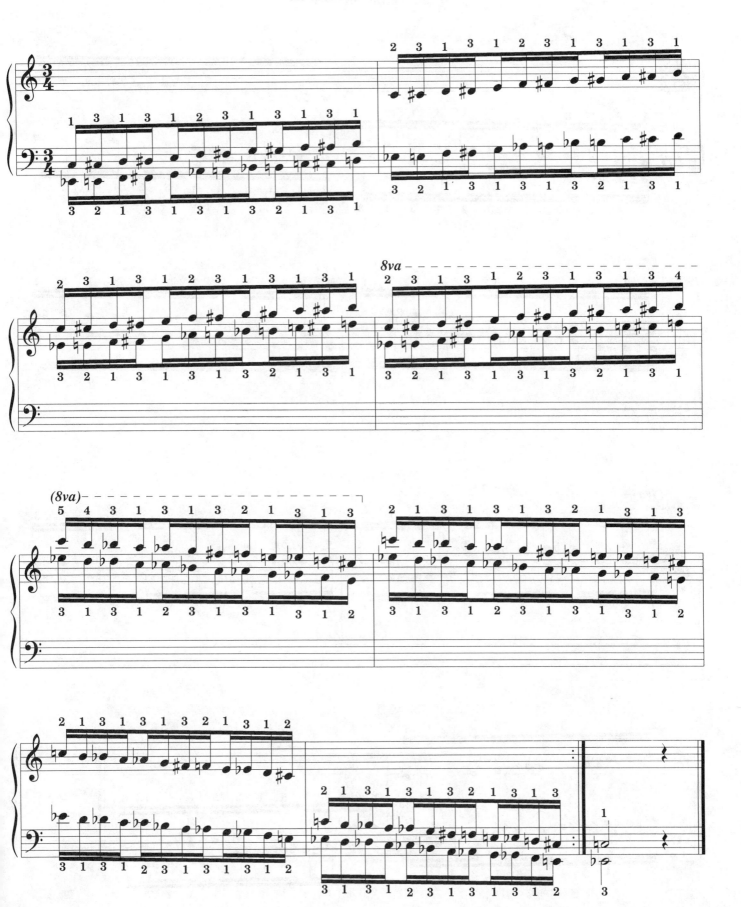

131

CHROMATIC SCALES
AT A MINOR SIXTH

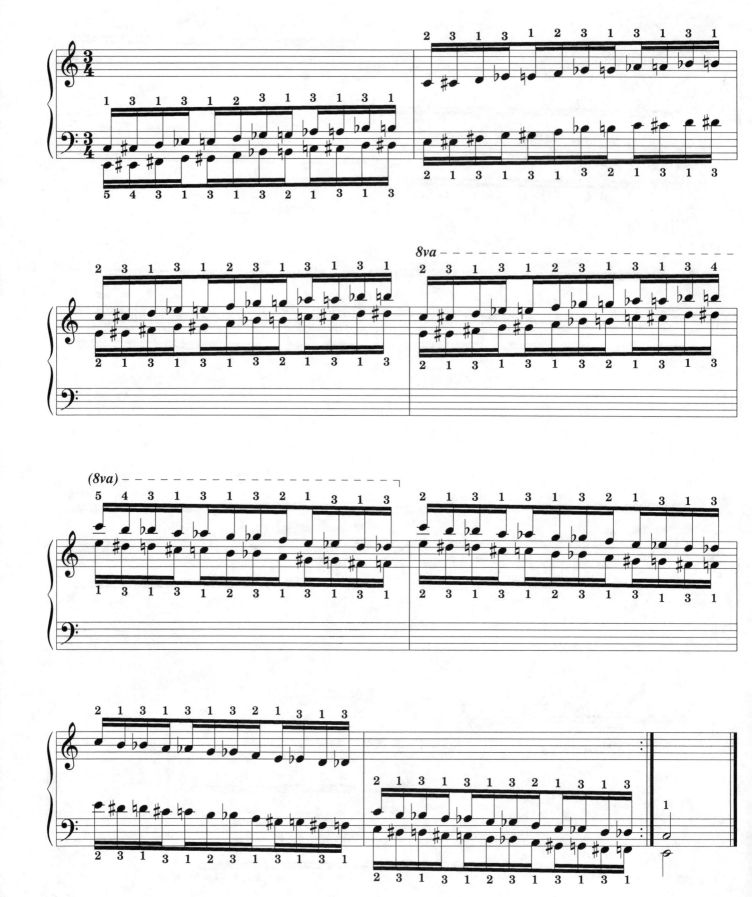

132

CHROMATIC STUDY FOR THE RIGHT HAND

Hermann Berens

CHROMATIC STUDY FOR THE LEFT HAND

Hermann Berens

Scales in Double Thirds

Play legato at a moderate tempo at first. Increase speed gradually.

C major

C minor

G major

G minor

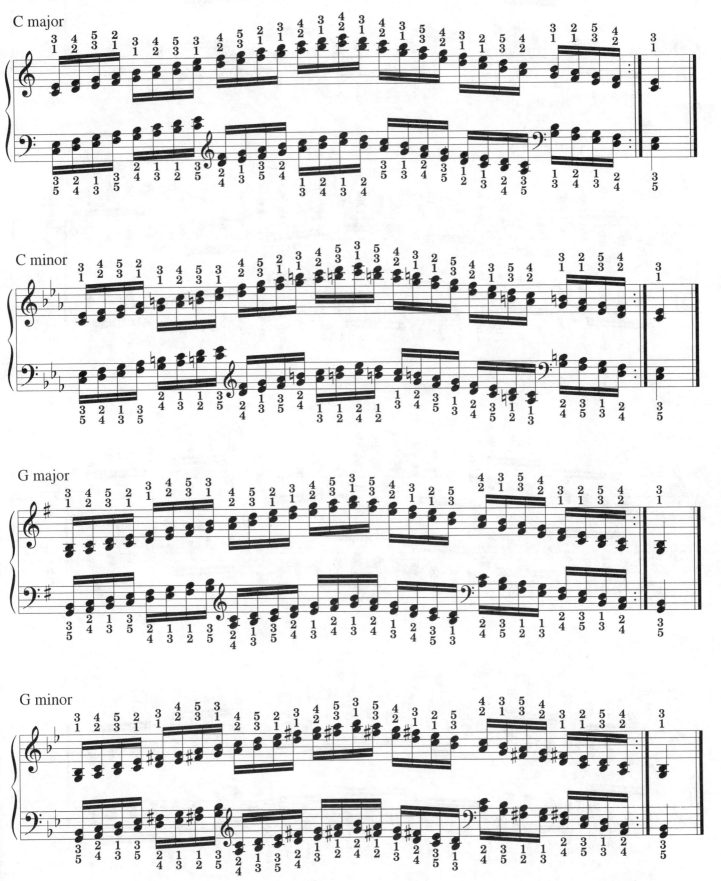

D major

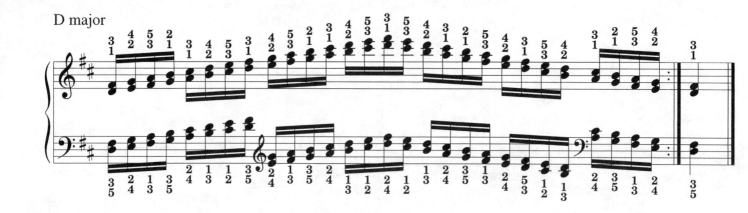

D minor

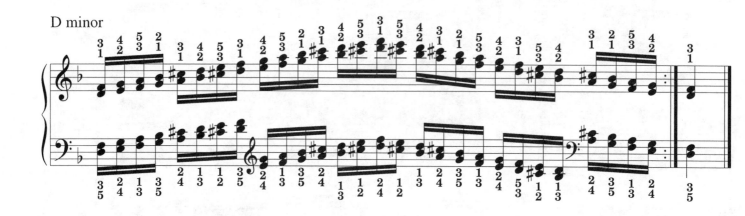

A major

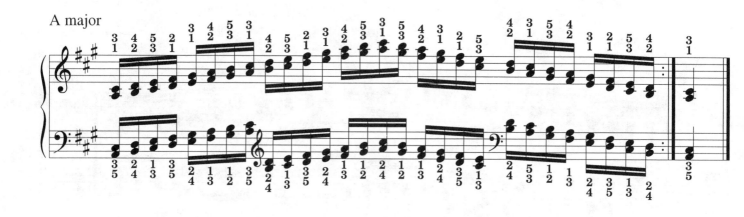

A minor

E major

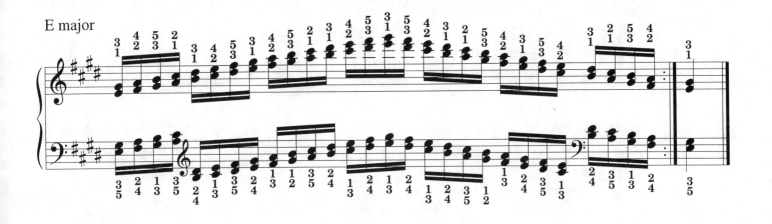

E minor

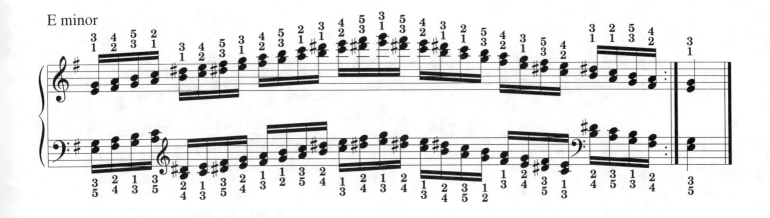

B major

B minor

F♯ major

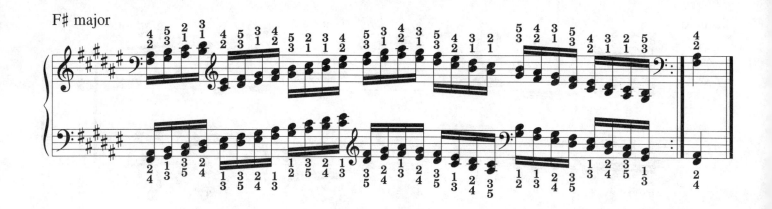

F♯ minor

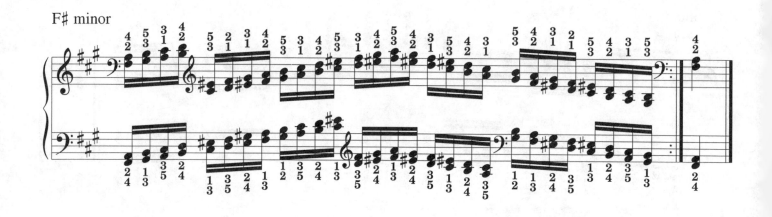

C♯ major

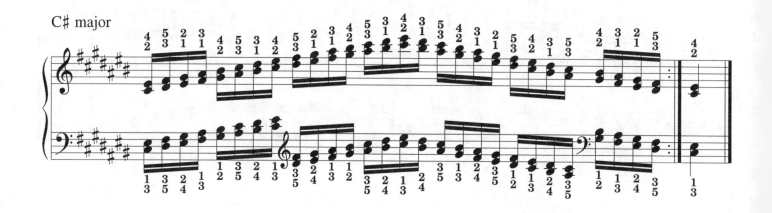

C♯ minor

Ab major

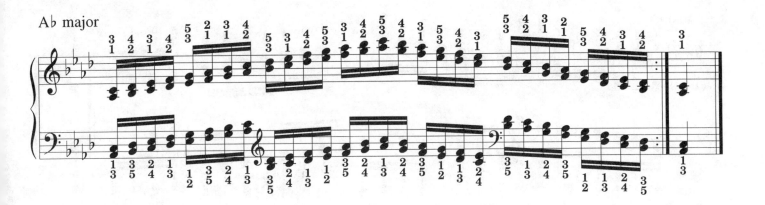

Ab minor

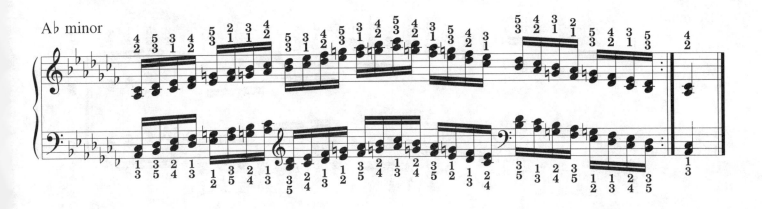

Eb major

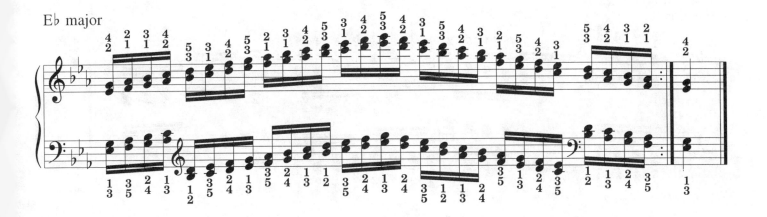

Eb minor

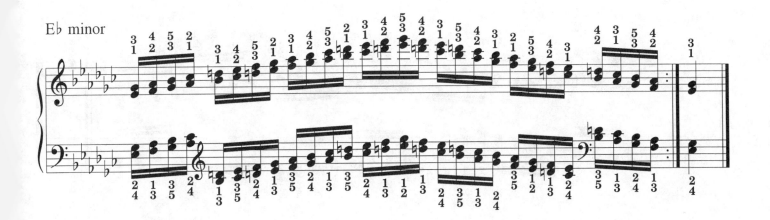

B♭ major

B♭ minor

F major

F minor

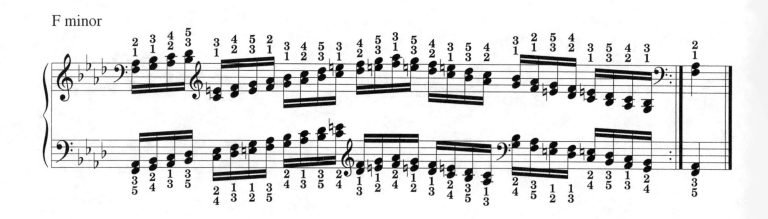

140

Chromatic Scales in Double Minor Thirds

TRILLS IN THIRDS
Op. 740, No.34

Carl Czerny

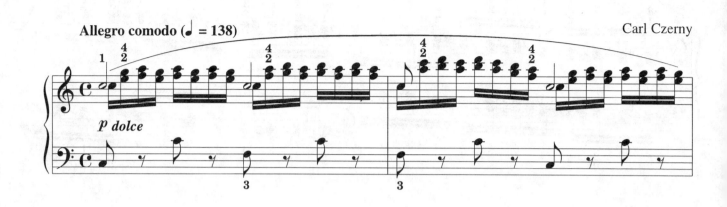

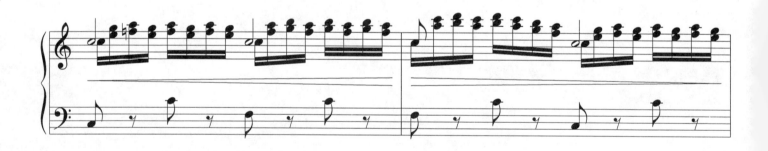

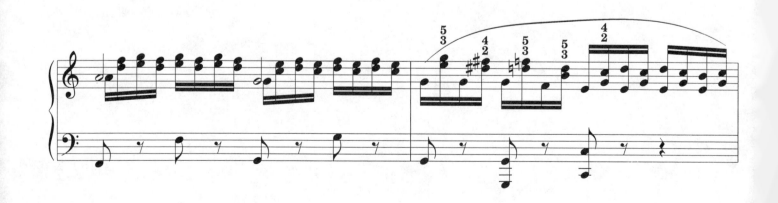

EXERCISE IN THIRDS
OP. 740, No. 10

Carl Czerny

Legato Third Exercise

from Gradus ad Parnassum

Muzio Clementi

151

154

THIRDS & SECONDS EXERCISE

FROM 51 EXERCISES

Johannes Brahms

RIGHT HAND EXERCISE

Legato double-note figures in the right hand

MODULATING SEQUENCE FOR HEAVY CHORD PRACTICE

Three ways of practicing this exercise are equally useful (examples of which follow). The braces signify that the keys are to be struck and the tones produced simultaneously; the curved lines signify that tones are to be spread or played as arpeggios.

E.M. Bowman

NO. 112 Exercise

Selections from "Sixty Studies of Pischna"

Preparatory exercises

Practice in all keys

J.Pischna

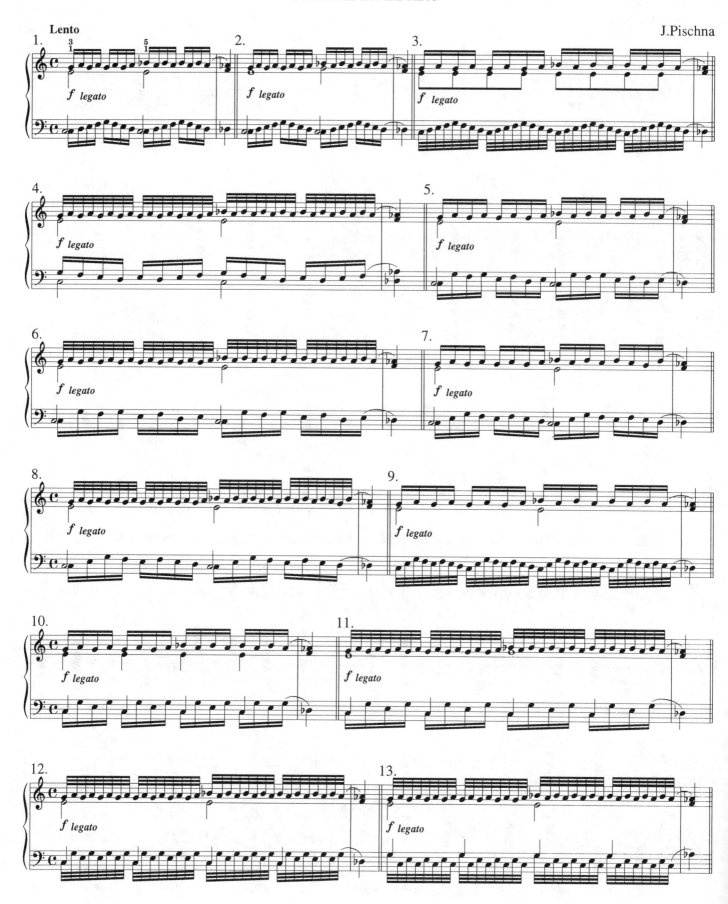

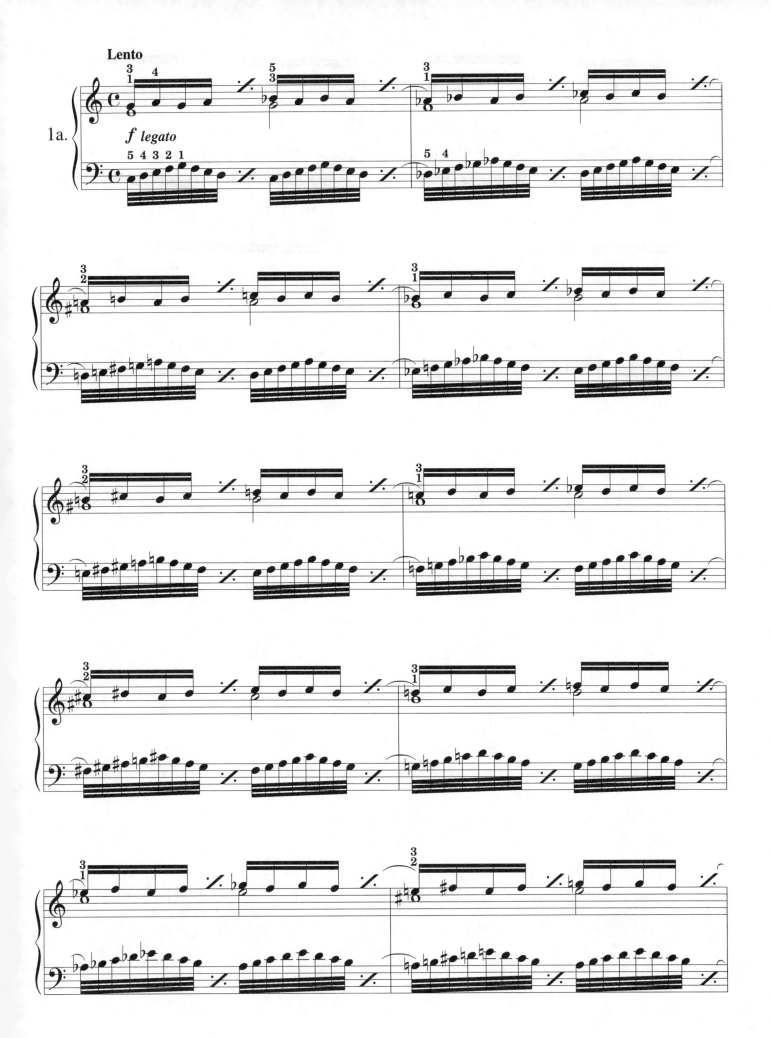

PREPARATORY EXERCISES TO NO. 7

PRACTICE IN ALL KEYS

Pischna

161

PREPARATORY EXERCISES TO No. 29

PRACTICE IN ALL KEYS

Pischna

Preparatory Exercises to No. 31

Practice in All Keys

Pischna

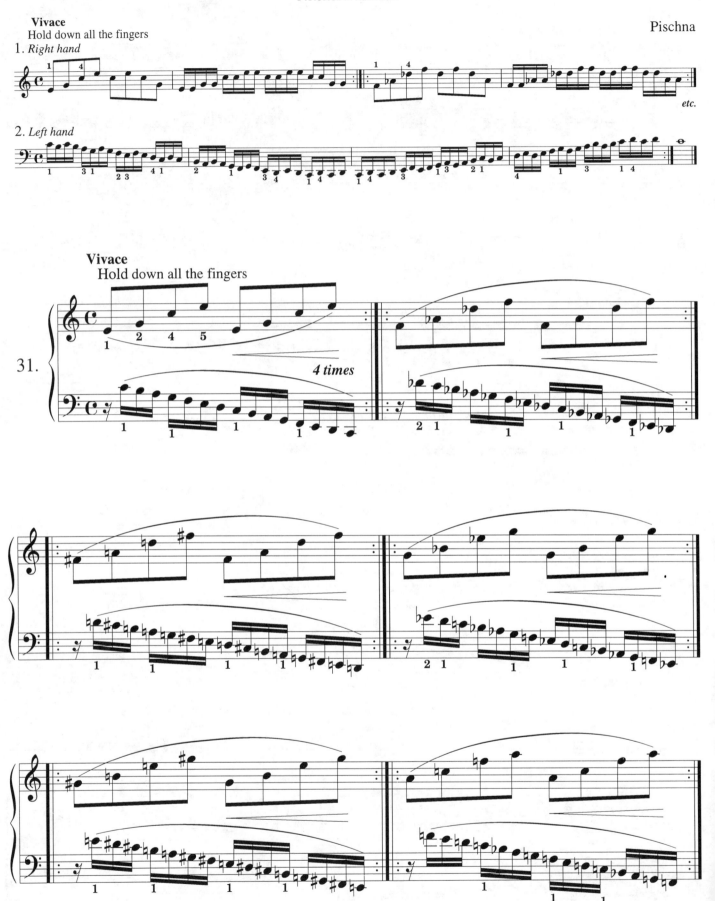

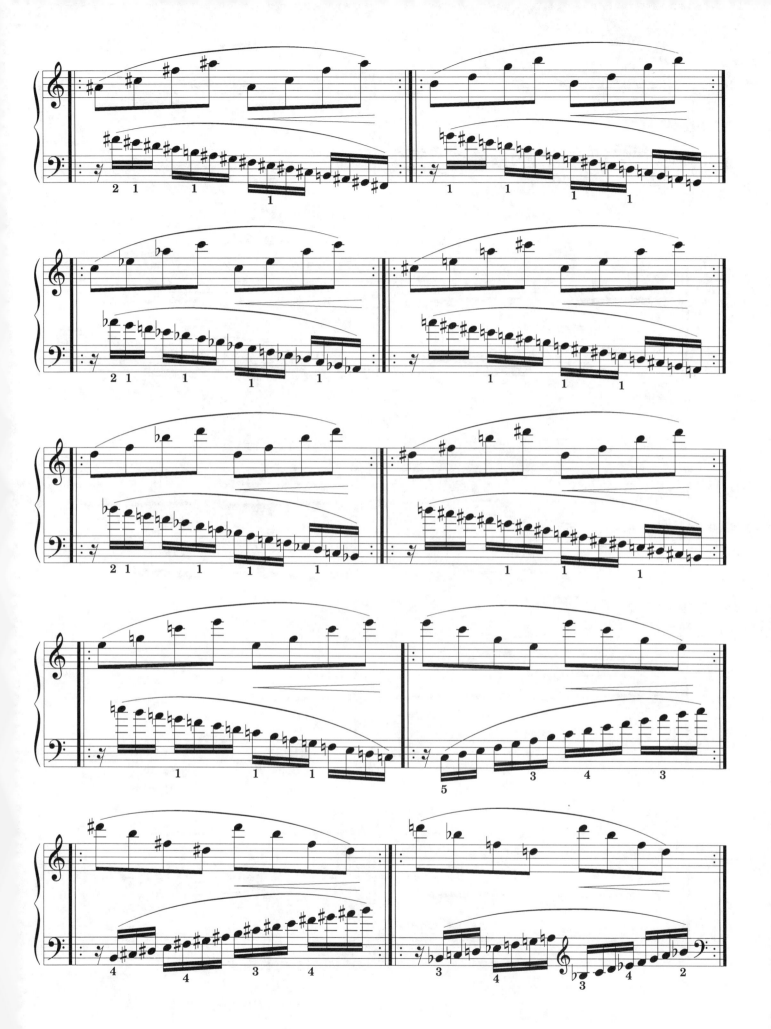

165

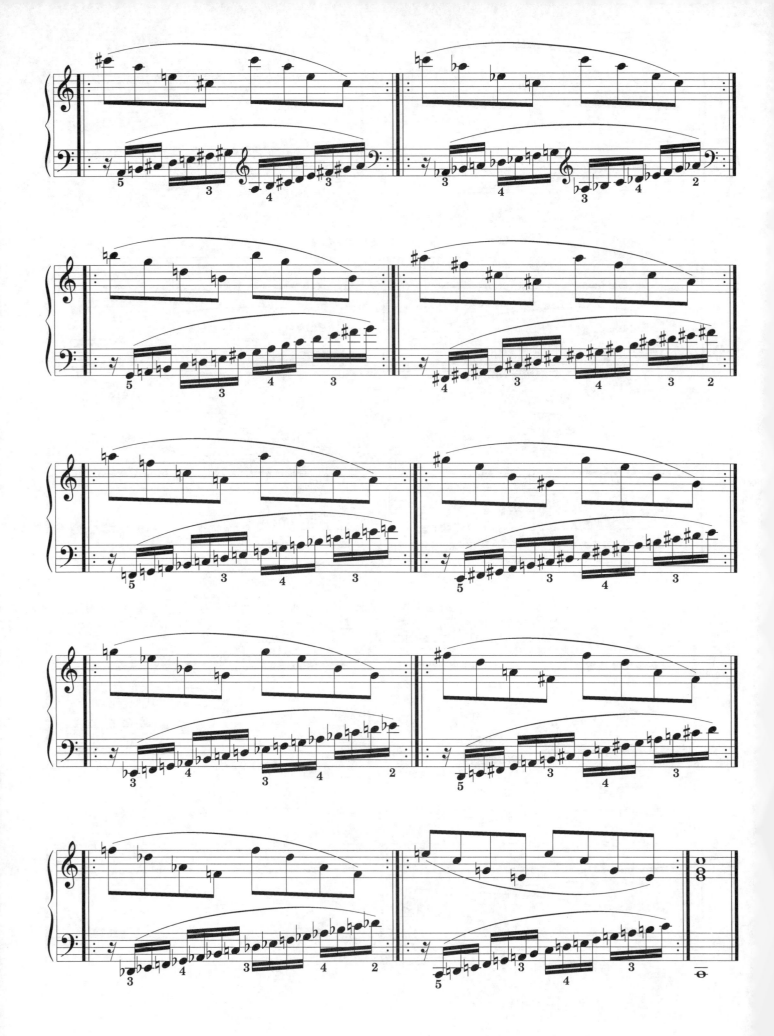

CONTRARY OCTAVE EXERCISE

Pischna

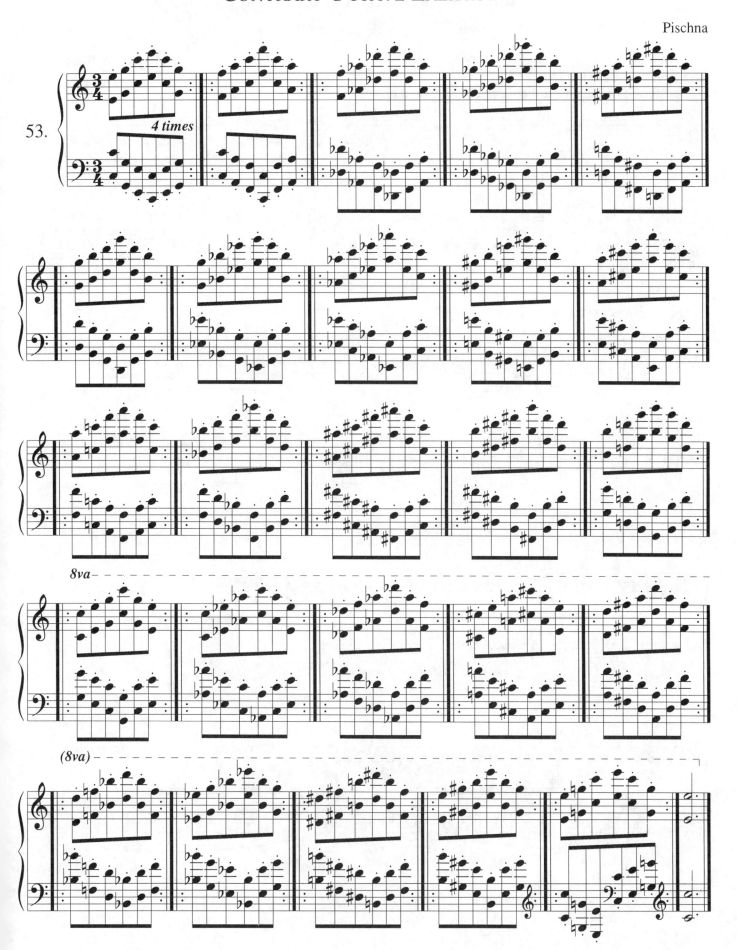

OCTAVE EXERCISES FROM *"TOUCH AND TECHNIC"*

by William Mason

Rotary Exercises in Octaves
To be played by each hand alternately, the left hand playing in a lower octave.

Right hand

Left hand

Compass of three octaves

Compass of three octaves

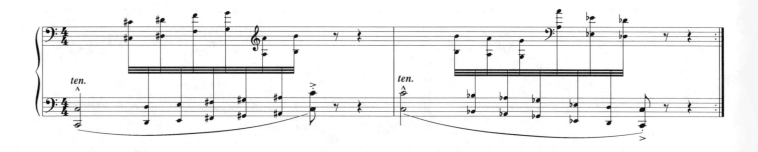

School of Octave Playing
Book I
Exercises

Isidor Philipp

In all major and minor keys

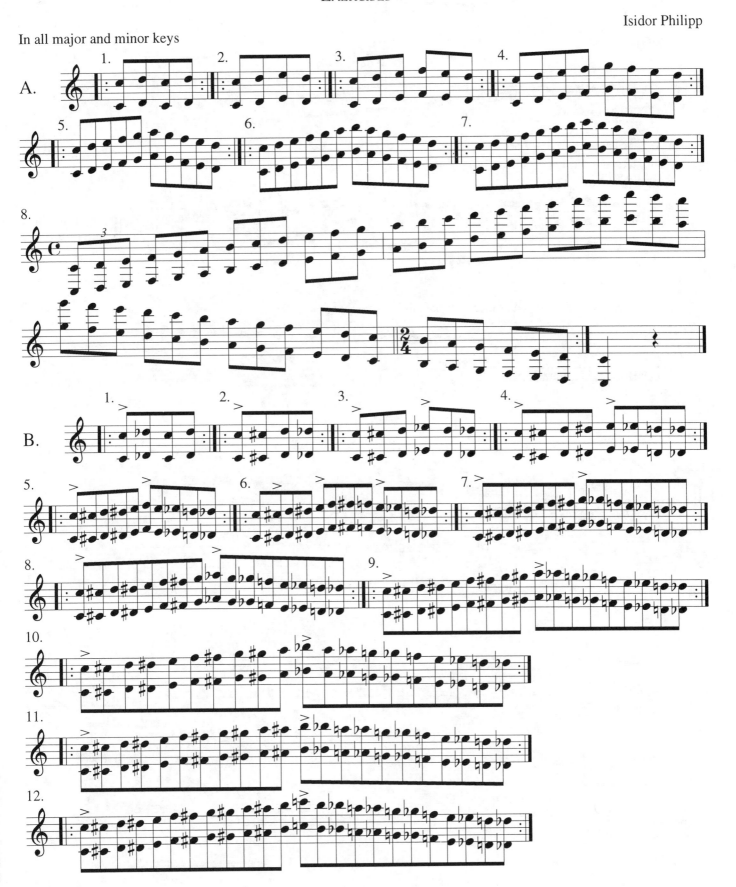

13.

(8va)- - - - - - - -

Repeat 4 times.
(♩ = 104 - 120)

1.

C. -in all major and minor keys.

The above exercise, *legato*. The same exercise, in broken chords.

2.

3.

4.

(left hand to play an octave higher.)

5.

6. Different rhythms.

7.

8.

9.

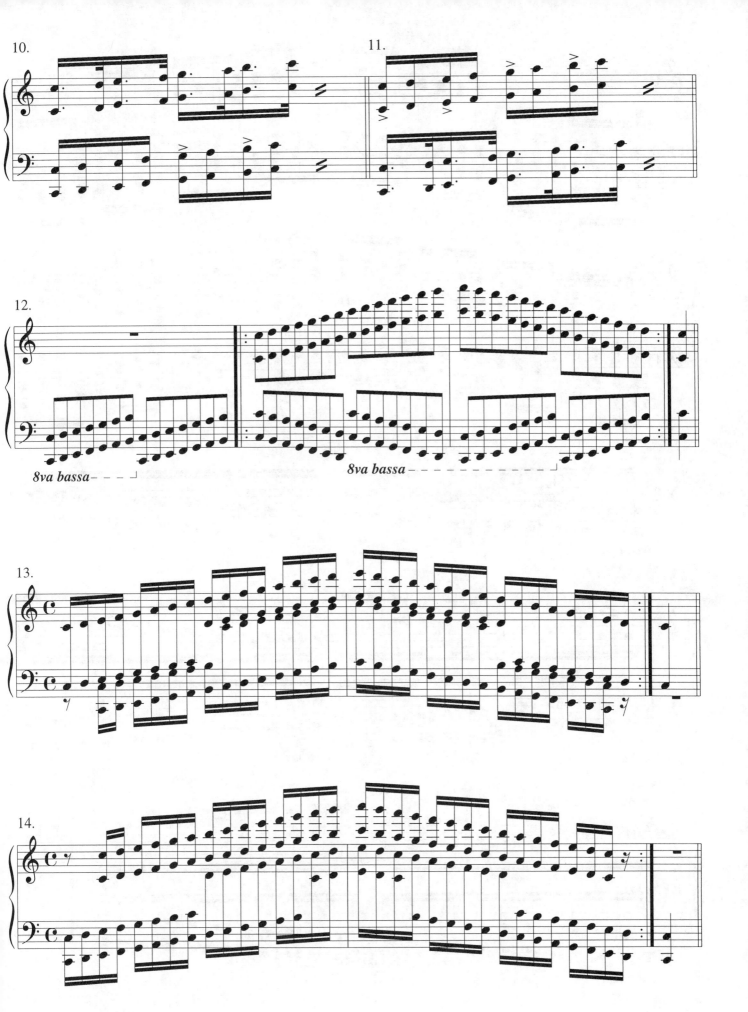

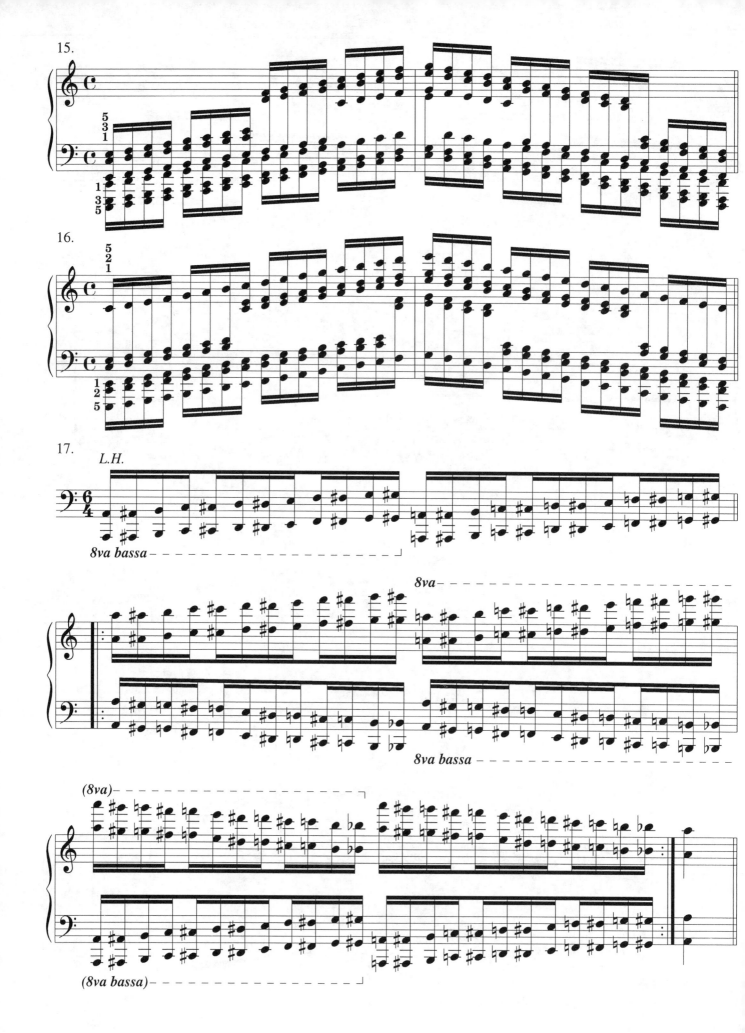

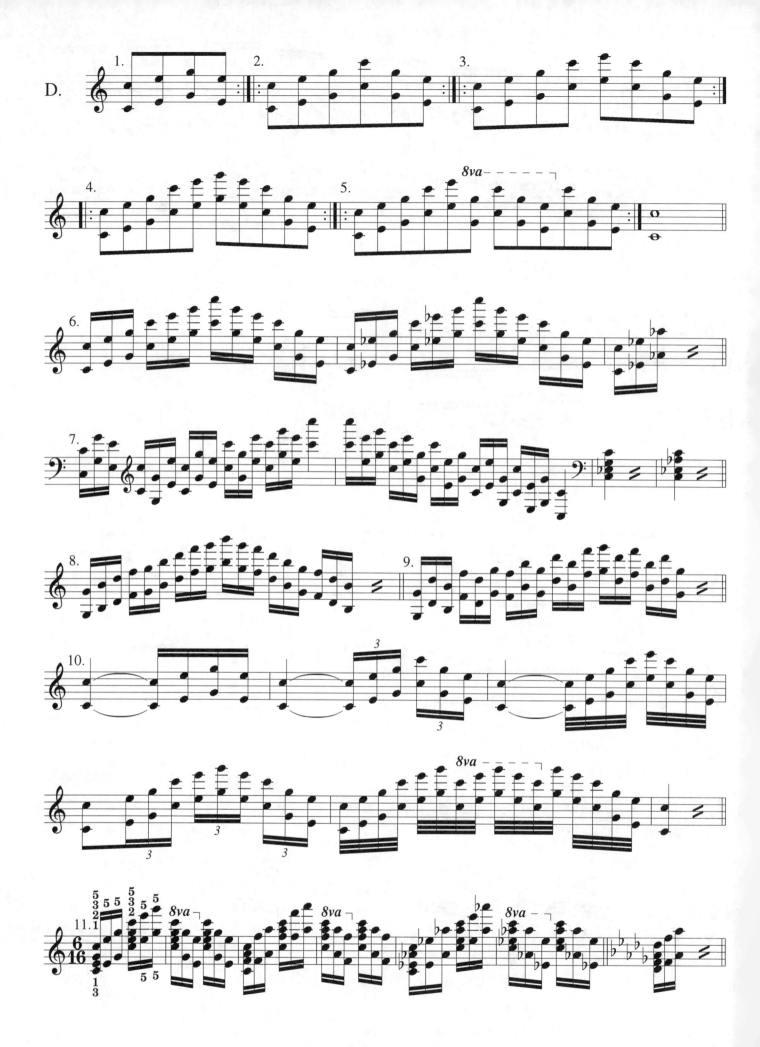

174

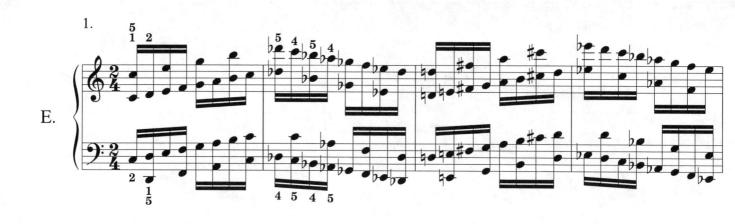

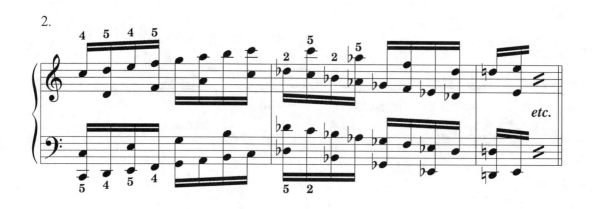

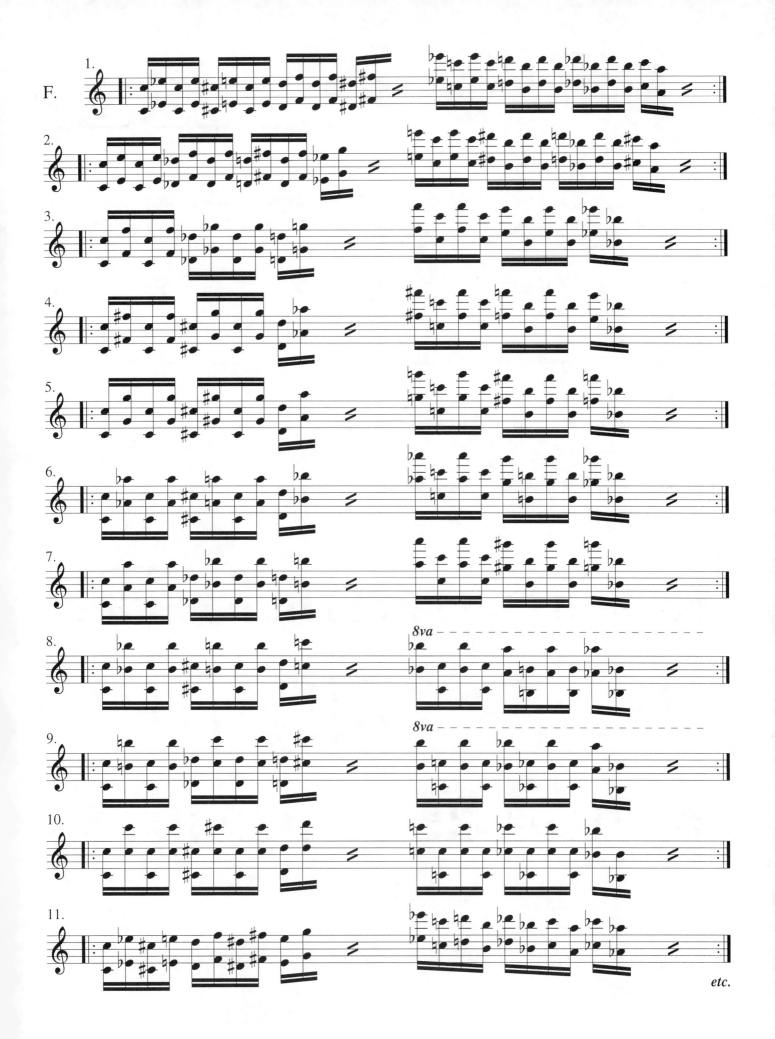

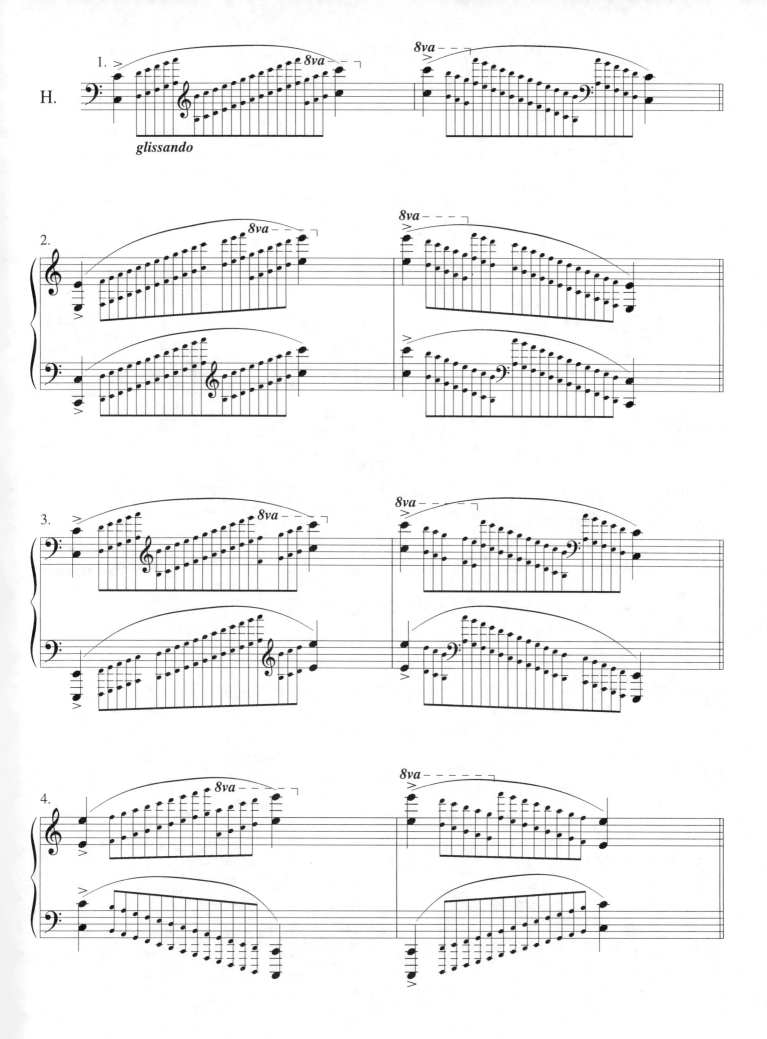

OCTAVE STUDY
Op. 188, No. 1

Bernhard Wolff

STACCATO OCTAVE ETUDE

ALLA TARANTELLA
Staccato octave passages

Josef Löw

184

OCTAVE STUDY IN THE FORM OF FUGUE
OP. 78, NO. 1

I. Philipp

* Theme after Bach.

ARPEGGIO OF THE DIMINISHED SEVENTH

EXERCISES FOR INDEPENDENCE OF THE FINGERS
EXAMPLE OF MODULATION

I. Philipp

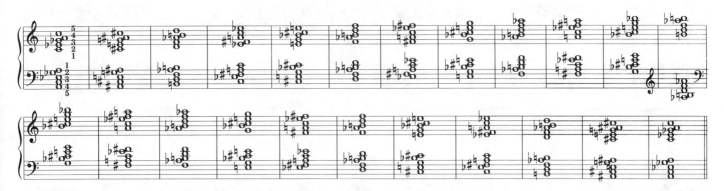

All exercises are to be transposed, following the illustration given above. Practise slowly, with a very supple arm, and strong finger-action, depressing each key to the bottom with a full, round and even tone.

Only the two first harmonic forms of each exercise are given, the remaining ten transpositions having to be thought out by the player, who is by this means prevented from practising in that dull, mechanical way which so often acts disastrously on the musical instincts of even the most gifted. With this simple material, _ and brains, _ with patience, conscientiousness, and careful attention, one will infallibly acquire in a short time, absolute independence of the fingers.

1st Series

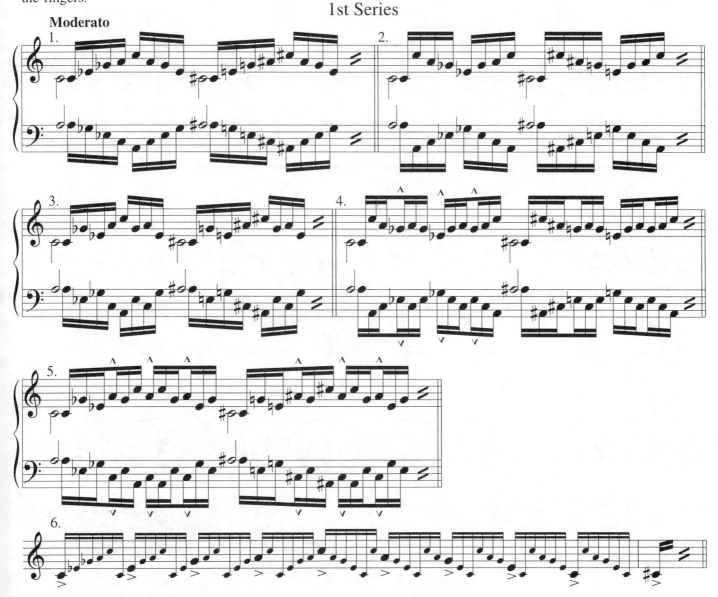

Moderato

6th Series

(Practise in parallel motion, and also in contrary motion.)

Allegretto *

* Fingerings for the left hand marked below the notes, and for the right, above them.

** *p.m.* = parallel motion; *c.m.* = contrary motion—Always take the Example of Modulation as a model (for the left hand) and begin with this chord:

Conclusion

1. Molto lento e pesante

2. Molto lento e pesante *(from the wrist.)*

Fugue in C

Johann Sebastian Bach